LECTURES IN
INTERNATIONAL FINANCE

Crisis, Coordination, Currency Unions, and Debt

Paul R Masson

University of Toronto, Canada

LECTURES IN INTERNATIONAL FINANCE

Crisis, Coordination, Currency Unions, and Debt

World Scientific

NEW JERSEY · LONDON · SINGAPORE · BEIJING · SHANGHAI · HONG KONG · TAIPEI · CHENNAI

Published by

World Scientific Publishing Co. Pte. Ltd.

5 Toh Tuck Link, Singapore 596224

USA office: 27 Warren Street, Suite 401-402, Hackensack, NJ 07601

UK office: 57 Shelton Street, Covent Garden, London WC2H 9HE

Library of Congress Cataloging-in-Publication Data
Masson, Paul R.
   Lectures in international finance : crisis, coordination, currency unions, and debt / by Paul
R. Masson.
     p. cm.
Includes bibliographical references and index.
ISBN-13 978-981-256-911-0 -- ISBN-10 981-256-911-1
ISBN-13 978-981-256-912-7 (pbk) -- ISBN-10 981-256-912-X (pbk.)
   1. International finance. 2. Monetary policy. I. Title.

HG3881.M356 2007
332'.042--dc22

                       2006042119

British Library Cataloguing-in-Publication Data
A catalogue record for this book is available from the British Library.

Typeset by Stallion Press
Email: enquiries@stallionpress.com

Printed in Singapore by World Scientific Printers (S) Pte Ltd

Contents

Part II   International Economic Policy Coordination   61

4.   Is Policy Coordination Desirable?   63

5.   Sustaining Coordination   76

Part III   Common Currency Areas   85

6.   Monetary Integration   87

Preface

This book has evolved from lectures given to graduate students at the University of Toronto. The four topics treated, currency crises and contagion, international economic policy coordination, currency unions, and sovereign debt, are central to international macroeconomics and finance. Thus, every student in this field should be familiar with the principal models in these four areas, and be able to work through their derivation and understand their implications. The purpose of this book is to provide students a basis for doing so, as well as explaining the relevance of the various models to events in the international monetary and financial system. The book includes discussion of a number of episodes, where the models help to understand events — in particular the currency crises of the 1990s, episodes of monetary policy coordination among G-7 countries, the tension between monetary and fiscal policies within the euro zone, and third world debt issues. In this I draw on my experience at the International Monetary Fund, which was in the front line of the 1980s debt crisis and the 1990s currency crises, and at the OECD during the 1970s and early 1980s, when that institution played an important role in giving advice on international economic policy coordination to its member countries. I also contributed to the IMF's policy advice to countries that were members of currency unions, principally the euro zone and the CFA franc zone in Africa.

The book is aimed at graduate students who have studied international macroeconomics and are familiar with calculus and game theory. In addition, it is hoped that practitioners who want a unified treatment of the models of international finance and a discussion of their relevance to the major events of the last half century in the international financial arena will find this book useful.

Acknowledgement

I am grateful to my University of Toronto graduate students who have showed such enthusiasm for my course, and especially to Xiaolu Wang who has carefully checked through the text. Michael Chui and Demosthenes Tambakis have kindly given me comments on the book. I would like to thank the co-authors of my papers whose material is adapted for use in the book, in particular Xavier Debrun, Allan Drazen, Atish Ghosh, Olivier Jeanne, and Catherine Pattillo. However, neither they nor the others mentioned above should be held responsible for remaining errors. Finally, I would like to thank the staff at World Scientific for their excellent support.

Introduction

0.1. Plan of the Book

The last half century has been an exciting time for those studying international monetary and financial economics. Dramatic events in the international arena have driven research into the topics of this book. The Bretton Woods System of fixed but adjustable exchange rate parities, initially anchored to gold (given the United States' commitment to a fixed price of $35/ounce), and later just centred on the US currency (after the closing of the US Treasury's gold "window"), broke down in 1973 after a series of crises. However, pegged exchange rates were not completely abandoned, and several waves of currency crises have occurred subsequently, especially during the 1980s and 1990s. Much attention was focussed on understanding the causes of crises and trying to predict their timing, and formal crisis models were developed. Unfortunately, each new set of crises that occurred differed in major respects from the predictions of existing models, so these models were refined and extended. The first part of the book details these models, explains their relevance, and identifies their limitations.

Since the breakdown of Bretton Woods, each of the major international currencies (now the US dollar, the euro, and the yen) has floated with respect to the others, sometimes in ways that have seemed undesirable. Moreover, the world economy was hit by major shocks in the 1970s and early 1980s related to the high world oil price, productivity slowdown, and unsustainable fiscal policies, hence the practical interest in the coordination of monetary and fiscal policies among the major industrial countries. The high points of such macroeconomic coordination were the 1978 Bonn summit and the Plaza Agreement and Louvre Accord of the mid-1980s. The academic literature attempted formally to model the process of coordination, understand under what circumstances it might be desirable, and identify cases when it could in fact be counterproductive. This is the second topic treated in the book.

Though the breakdown in Bretton Woods introduced an era of exchange rate flexibility, which was seen in some quarters to have decisive advantages, there continued to be a search for ways to reduce the harmful effects of exchange rate variability. This effort led to the creation of the European Monetary System in 1979 and ultimately the introduction of the euro in 1999, which has replaced the currencies of the zone's member countries. It has also stimulated continuing interest in monetary union projects in other parts of the world. While academic work in this area has a number of dimensions — and indeed Robert Mundell's work preceded the practical planning for EMU — our interest in this volume is on recent work that attempts to understand the interaction of a single monetary policy with decentralised (national) fiscal policies in a monetary union. The models we study, a very active area of current research, are largely inspired by the debate within Europe over the dangers of excessive deficits and high accumulated debt, and the attempt to refine the euro area's Stability and Growth Pact.

Our final topic is sovereign debt, that is, the borrowing on international capital markets by sovereign governments. Interest in analysis of this topic became strong as a result of the third-world debt crisis in the 1980s when there were widespread defaults and an almost complete drying up of new lending to developing countries, with resulting low investment and slow growth — making the 1980s a "lost decade" for many of these countries. This episode inspired research into the reasons banks and other investors would lend at all to foreign governments, given that their recourse against the country was limited in the case of default — unlike domestic debtors, where the legal system prescribed various remedies. This literature continues to be relevant, given the astonishing revival of lending to developing countries — with occasional breaks associated with crisis periods. Current research discussed in this part of the book includes mechanisms to improve the institutional framework for lending to developing countries, both to prevent crises and to facilitate capital flows to countries with profitable investment opportunities.

While these four topics do not exhaust the field, they are at the centre of the academic literature in international finance and of the preoccupations of policymakers and market practitioners. As such, a thorough grounding in the models enhances understanding of the forces at work in the international monetary and financial system.

The four parts of the book are self-contained, so that the topics, though inter-related, can in fact be studied separately. Clearly, policy coordination, Part II, is also relevant to Part III, the interaction of monetary and fiscal policies. And currency crises, Part I, are often associated with debt crises, discussed under Part IV. But they need not be studied sequentially.

The text works through models that are largely taken from the published, academic literature, making only a few changes to the original notation where necessary to eliminate inconsistencies. There is no attempt to develop a single dynamic, optimising framework of which each of the models would be a subcase — this is clearly too difficult a task, and even if it were possible, it would hide in complexity the key features and insights of each of the models.

The models, moreover, need to be understood in the light of the real-world events alluded to above. In particular, the strengths and weaknesses of each model emerge when discussing the various crises and coordination episodes. Just as the models were inspired by events in the global monetary and financial arena, their relevance needs to be evaluated on that basis.

0.2. Some Basic Concepts

0.2.1. *Channels of interdependence*

Different economies are linked to each other through various channels. They trade with each other, importing and exporting goods and services — though some goods and, especially, services are not traded, either because they need to be consumed near to where they are produced (perishable goods, or personal services like haircuts) or because their price does not justify the cost of transport. Countries also export and import capital, that is, financial transactions between domestic and foreign residents take place. Capital flows are classified in various ways: direct investment flows (where the investor has some control over the asset, for instance, because it involves establishing or expanding a subsidiary in a foreign country) versus portfolio flows, or debt versus equity flows, or commercial versus official financing. Official financing (other than export credits, which are very short term) applies principally to the lending by richer countries and international financial institutions (the International Monetary Fund, the World Bank, and Regional Development Banks) to poorer countries, in the form of either grants or "concessional lending" (that is, loans granted at a rate of interest below the commercial rate). In contrast, the middle-income developing countries typically have access to a variety of commercial financing, in the form of bank loans or bonds issued on international capital markets. In addition to trade and capital flows, countries may be linked through migration and the remittances of workers back to their home countries. Though migration is subject to many restrictions, both trade and capital flows have benefited from international efforts at liberalisation. In particular, the General Agreement on Tariffs and Trade and its successor, the World Trade Organisation, have engineered reductions in tariffs and non-tariff barriers that hindered trade in goods and services. Capital mobility is not viewed as unambiguously desirable, but because of the inefficiencies created by capital controls and the difficulty in enforcing them, there has been a progressive abandonment of those controls. Only developing countries retain significant capital controls, and even for those countries their prevalence is much less now than in previous decades.

The interdependence that results from countries exploiting beneficial trading opportunities (e.g., from selling their production at prices that exceed those available domestically or from borrowing capital abroad to invest profitably at home) also creates the possibility of external crises and of unfavourable spillovers from policies adopted abroad. This in turn opens the door to potential gains from international economic policy coordination. Policy coordination can in principle allow countries to achieve higher welfare by joint action than by acting independently.

0.2.2. *The balance of payments and the money supply*

The overall balance of payments measures the net effect on a country's holdings of foreign exchange reserves of its transactions with the rest of the world. The balance of payments is broken down into the current account and the capital account. The **current account** includes transactions related to trade in goods and services; services include such things as tourism, insurance and banking services, and payments of interest and dividends on foreign lending and borrowing. The **capital account** refers to trade in assets, that is, purchases and sales of bonds, loans, and equity shares. As its name implies, the balance of payments "balances": the change in foreign exchange reserves (ΔR) equals the current account balance (CA) plus the capital account balance (KA):

$$\Delta R = CA + KA.$$

If a country does not intervene (because it engages in a "pure float" — see below) so that the change of reserves equals zero, then the current account balance must exactly equal the negative of the capital account balance:

$$CA = -KA.$$

Thus, in this case a surplus in one account must be matched by a deficit in the other.

Foreign exchange reserves are held in international currencies (principally the US dollar, but increasingly in euros) or gold. Gold, however, has diminished greatly in importance since it no longer serves as an anchor for exchange rates nor as a vehicle for intervention. Foreign exchange reserves can be used to cushion an economy from temporary shocks to its current and capital accounts. However, they are also important because they are a component of the *domestic* money supply. We can see this from a simplified balance sheet of the central bank. The central bank issues domestic currency (its liability), while on the asset side it holds foreign exchange reserves and claims on the government or other domestic entities (commercial banks or non-financial companies). Thus, a stylised central bank balance sheet equates the domestic money supply (M) to reserves and net domestic credit (D):

$$M = D + R.$$

This identity serves as the basis for the **monetary theory of the balance of payments**, which argues that the causality goes in a fixed exchange rate regime from domestic credit expansion (ΔD) in excess of the increase in money demand (ΔM) to a fall in reserves ($\Delta R < 0$). The identity also helps to understand why an exogenous increase in reserves (for instance, because of a surge in capital inflows or resource revenues) may have inflationary consequences: unless D falls, an increase in R will increase the money supply, and, for given output, will therefore tend to raise prices.

0.2.3. *Exchange rate regimes*

If a country has its own currency, then a key price is its **exchange rate** against some international currency chosen as numeraire. The country may choose to maintain a fixed exchange rate against that numeraire (or against a basket of currencies or against a commodity), or instead, allow the exchange rate to fluctuate. That is, the country may have a **fixed rate regime** or a **floating rate regime**. In practice, countries seldom have perfectly fixed (that is, immutably set) or perfectly flexible exchange rates (the latter would involve no changes in foreign exchange reserves as a result of official intervention). Exchange rate regimes can be situated somewhere along the continuum between those two extremes. **Currency boards**, in which there is an automatic mechanism linking the money supply to changes in reserves with no possibility of domestic credit expansion, are close to the perfectly fixed extreme; however, as Argentina's abandonment of its currency board in 2002 showed, even such a regime may not be immutable. The earlier gold standard (abandoned in 1914) pegged most currencies to the value of gold. A weaker arrangement of fixed exchange rates, the Bretton Woods System, prevailed from the end of the Second World War to 1973. It provided for fixed exchange rates between currencies with occasional adjustment of parities in response to fundamental payments imbalances. The Exchange Rate Mechanism of the European Monetary System (1979–1998) similarly involved adjustable parities but wider bands of fluctuation around those parities. A successor to that arrangement defines bands of fluctuation relative to the euro for the currencies of some of the EU countries that are not yet members of the euro zone.

The advantages of fixed exchange rates include the benefits of exchange rate stability, but there are costs deriving from the lack of flexibility to respond to domestic developments. In particular, if a country faces high capital mobility a fixed exchange rate makes an independent monetary policy impossible.

Countries may choose to abandon their own currency, thus getting the full benefits from lower transactions costs of using an international currency. The two principal forms this may take are **dollarisation**, that is, the unilateral adoption of another country's currency (this term is general and is not restricted to the use of the dollar), and membership in a **currency union**, that is, a multilateral arrangement involving the shared responsibility among member countries for the operations of the central bank that issues the currency. The principal examples of currency unions in the world at present are the euro zone (in which some European Union countries share a common currency), the CFA franc zone in Africa, and the Eastern Caribbean Currency Union.

0.2.4. *Real versus nominal exchange rates and parity conditions*

The **nominal exchange rate** is simply the number of units of one currency needed to buy another. The **real exchange rate** also takes into account the price levels in the two countries, and conceptually it measures the rate of exchange of goods of one country against goods of another. Thus, if S is the nominal (spot) rate, expressed as units of local currency per dollar, P is the domestic price level, and P^* is the US price level, then the country's real exchange rate Z against the dollar is

$$Z = P^*S/P.$$

It should be noted that in keeping with the usual convention an increase in either S or Z constitutes a **depreciation** (nominal or real, respectively): more of the domestic currency (or more real goods) are needed to purchase a given amount of foreign currency (or goods). **Purchasing power parity** (PPP) implies that real purchasing power stays constant, meaning that the real exchange rate does not change. This is usually interpreted as a long-run equilibrium condition linking the price levels of two countries and their nominal exchange rate. Indeed, if the real exchange rate is constant, $\Delta \ln Z = 0$, then we must have

$$\Delta \ln S = \Delta \ln P - \Delta \ln P^*.$$

Letting lower case letters stand for the logarithms of the respective upper case variables, PPP in relative terms (i.e., in difference form, presumably over a long period) can be written

$$\Delta s = \Delta p - \Delta p^*.$$

Note that PPP is not an identity but rather is based on a behavioural hypothesis that the real exchange rate returns to a constant value; there has been considerable empirical work testing whether this is true and, if so, over what horizon. That empirical work finds some support for PPP but concludes that adjustment to the PPP exchange rate is slow.

Interest rate parity links the difference between current and expected future exchange rates with the differential in interest rates. It is based on the hypothesis that the expected returns from holding assets of the same maturity in the two currencies should be the same. Suppose that the exchange rate that will prevail in some future period is known; call this S_{+1}, and that the corresponding-maturity interest rates in the home country and in the United States are i and i^*, respectively. It should be the case here (since there is no uncertainty) that

$$S_{+1}/S = \frac{1+i}{1+i^*}.$$

Thus, if the home currency is going to depreciate ($S_{+1} > S$), then an investor needs to be compensated for it by a higher interest rate than on US dollars ($i > i^*$). If we take logs, using s as above to stand for the log of the exchange rate, and approximate $\ln(1 + i)$ by i, we can write the above equation for interest rate parity as

$$s_{+1} - s = i - i^*.$$

In practice, the future spot rate is not known, and interest rate parity can take two forms. **Covered interest parity** (CIP) uses the forward rate (F), which is known when the transaction is made, in place of the future spot rate. So CIP implies

$$f - s = i - i^*.$$

Since there is no risk in the transaction, arbitrage should operate to make CIP hold, and this is confirmed by empirical work (indeed, foreign exchange dealers' quotes are calculated such that there are no arbitrage profits to be made). **Uncovered interest parity** (UIP) replaces the future spot rate by its currently expected value (indicated with an e superscript):

$$s_{+1}^e - s = i - i^*.$$

Note that UIP asserts that expected returns are equalised: the relationship embodies no risk premium. In practice, investors may need to be compensated for risk, and this might lead to rejection of UIP. Testing UIP necessarily involves a joint hypothesis about the formation of expectations. Empirical work has generally rejected UIP, but the reasons for the rejection are the object of a considerable literature and continuing controversy.

0.2.5.   *International financial institutions*

Because of interdependence, exchange rate regimes and international transactions have shared effects that make international cooperation in this area desirable. The International Monetary Fund (IMF) was set up to facilitate cooperation and to establish "rules of the game" for the international monetary system. Though the Bretton Woods

System with its focus on exchange rate pegs has been abandoned, the IMF still conducts surveillance over countries' macroeconomic policies to discourage undesirable spillovers and has a mandate to condemn countries engaging in "currency manipulation" that would give them unfair competitive advantage. Moreover, the IMF and the World Bank provide financing to countries with balance of payments problems, aiming both to decrease the likelihood of crises and to mitigate their consequences. Thus, both the IMF and the World Bank took a major role during the 1980s developing countries debt crisis by providing official financing and facilitating the restructuring of defaulted debt. With increasing private capital flows to the middle-income developing countries, however, financing from international financial institutions has declined in importance, as has the role of international financial institutions in resolving crises.

Part I
Currency Crisis Models

Chapter 1

The First Generation

1.1. Historical Background

The extensive literature on currency crisis models was stimulated by the post-Second-World-War history with exchange rates, under the Bretton Woods System of fixed but adjustable pegs to the US dollar, which prevailed from 1945 to 1973. Generally, the exchange rates of major currencies were very stable, but there were occasional large movements (Chart 1.1). While in theory the Bretton Woods System combined the advantages of exchange rate stability with the flexibility to correct "fundamental imbalances", in practice it had weaknesses, which eventually would lead to its abandonment.

There were three major problems with this regime. The first was a systemic problem, and concerned the role of the key currency country, the United States. For world liquidity to increase, the United States had to run balance of payments deficits, but doing so adversely affected the credibility of the US commitment to exchange dollars for gold on demand (abandoned in 1968 except for central banks, and for

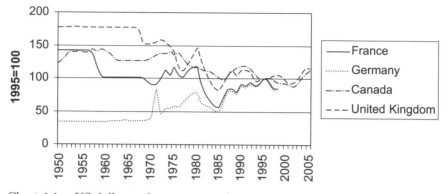

Chart 1.1.   US dollar exchange rates, selected countries.
Source: IMF, International Financial Statistics.

the latter in 1971). This dilemma was first analysed by Triffin (1960).
The second problem was that other countries sometimes operated
domestic policies that were incompatible with the commitment to a
peg. In particular, domestic credit expansion (often to finance government deficits) was too rapid, and this inconsistency made devaluation inevitable. Third, the Bretton Woods System was designed (in
1944) when capital flows were expected to remain severely restricted,
but increasing capital mobility made it easier for investors to profit
from anticipated exchange rate adjustments (or to avoid losses due
to domestic currency exposure). As a result, lack of credibility of
exchange rate pegs (due, for instance, to the inconsistent monetary
policies described above) led to speculative attacks. Some of these
failed, but if they succeeded they often pushed forward the time of
collapse of the peg. The central bank then either set a new depreciated value of the currency or allowed the currency to float. Notable
examples of exchange crises were the British pound's devaluation
of 1967, and that of the French franc in 1969, following unrest in
France during 1968. The devaluations in both countries were widely
expected, though their timing was uncertain. A devaluation of the
two countries' currencies became inevitable when foreign exchange
reserves declined to low levels (though they never reached zero).

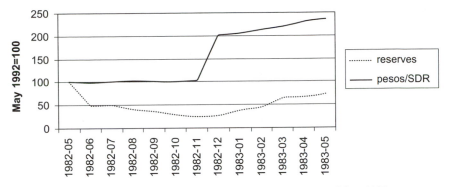

Chart 1.2. Mexico's reserves and exchange rate, May 1982–May 1983.
Source: IMF, International Financial Statistics.

First-generation currency crisis models focus on the path for foreign exchange reserves and the conditions that would lead to their exhaustion.

Though largely inspired by European experience, currency crisis models have even wider applicability to developing countries. While industrial countries have largely eschewed currency pegs and, except for EU countries, have embraced flexible exchange rates in the period since the breakdown of the Bretton Woods System, developing countries have typically avoided free floating of their currencies, preferring to limit flexibility through official or de facto pegs, typically to the US dollar. However, excessive domestic credit expansion has led to inflation rates that were higher than in the United States, and reserves eventually declined to minimum levels. Chart 1.2 illustrates the situation for Mexico in 1982–1983. By December 1982, reserves were almost exhausted; the authorities devalued the peso and then instituted a crawling peg with a steady devaluation. The improvement in international competitiveness caused reserves to rebound.

The first-generation models help explain when an attack will be successful, and predict its timing. They were initially inspired by models of extraction of exhaustible resources, and the seminal paper by Salant and Henderson (1978) considered when a peg for the price of gold would have to be adjusted as a response to depleting gold stocks. Krugman (1979) extended the model to exchange rates between currencies, in a general equilibrium framework of macroeconomic balance. The complications of his model have generally been avoided in later work, which has focused on money-market equilibrium and made simplifying assumptions that permit analytical solutions. Flood and Garber (1994) have gone furthest in formulating the first-generation model in a simple and elegant way that allows it to be applied to real-world data.

1.2.   The Flood–Garber Model

These authors make the following crucial assumptions, some of which are relaxed in later literature but are typical of most of the first-generation models:

- Money demand takes a simple form that depends on the price level and interest rate.
- Purchasing power parity (PPP) holds, and foreign prices are constant so that the domestic price level equals the exchange rate.
- Uncovered interest rate parity (UIP) holds (with the foreign interest rate constant), so expected exchange rate changes increase domestic interest rates one-for-one.
- Investors have perfect foresight.
- There is a lower bound to reserves.
- Domestic credit expansion is faster than money demand growth.

The first three assumptions allow a convenient linearisation. Let us first introduce notation:

$\quad M =$ the nominal money supply,

$\quad R =$ foreign exchange reserves,

$\quad D =$ domestic credit granted by the central bank (typically, to finance government spending),

$P(P^*) =$ the domestic (foreign) price level,

$$S = \text{the exchange rate (domestic currency value of}$$
$$\text{the foreign currency),}$$
$$i(i^*) = \text{domestic (foreign) interest rate.}$$

We use a dot over a variable to indicate its time derivative, that is, the rate of change in the variable over a time interval that goes to zero.

1.2.1. *Equations*

The model is based on some very simple building blocks that relate domestic prices and interest rates to the international economy, assumed exogenous.

$$M/P = a_0 - a_1 i, \tag{1.1}$$
$$M = R + D, \tag{1.2}$$
$$\dot{D} = \mu > 0, \tag{1.3}$$
$$P = P^* S, \tag{1.4}$$
$$i = i^* + \dot{S}/S. \tag{1.5}$$

The first equation is a simple form for money demand, which depends negatively on the interest rate and positively on the price level. Money supply, Equation (1.2), is backed by central bank holdings of foreign and domestic assets, and domestic credit, Equation (1.3), is simply assumed to grow at a constant rate. Equation (1.4) imposes PPP so that domestic prices are simply equal to the (exogenous) foreign price level converted at the current exchange rate. Finally, UIP links the domestic rate to the foreign rate plus the expected rate of change of the exchange rate. However, here there is no uncertainty, so the actual and expected changes are equal.

Equations (1.1), (1.4), and (1.5) yield

$$M = P^* S \left[a_0 - a_1 \left(i^* + \dot{S}/S \right) \right] = \beta S - \alpha \dot{S}, \tag{1.6}$$

where $\beta \equiv P^*(a_0 - a_1 i^*)$, and $\alpha \equiv a_1 P^*$, and it is assumed that $\beta > 0$.

Under a fixed exchange rate regime, with the parity indicated by a bar over the exchange rate, $S = \overline{S}$ and $\dot{S} = 0$.

Thus, in this case money **demand** is fixed, $M = \beta \overline{S}$, but money supply is given by $M = R + D$. Money-market equilibrium implies $\dot{R} = -\dot{D} = -\mu$.

Thus, reserves decline continuously, and since by assumption there is a lower bound to R, a collapse is inevitable. But when? It is here that the first-generation model gives some interesting insights. They are illustrated in Figure 1.1.

The point to be noted is that if the collapse did not occur until $\overline{T} = R(0)/\mu$, then there would be excess profits due to the discrete jump in the exchange rate. Why? Because at this time, suddenly the exchange rate floats and starts depreciating by an amount related to the rate of credit expansion, μ. We can see that if there is a steady depreciation (with $\ddot{S} = 0$), from (1.6),

$$\dot{S} = \frac{1}{\beta}\dot{M} = \frac{\mu}{\beta}.$$

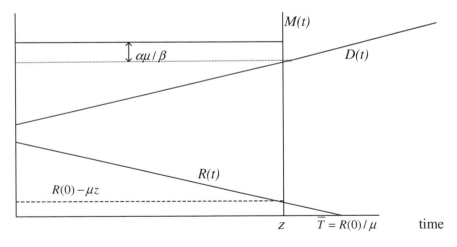

Figure 1.1.   Domestic credit, reserves, and the time of a successful attack.

But this depreciation means that agents would want to hold less money (because it has started depreciating continuously in value), implying that money demand would shift down by αS. At this point it is useful to consider possible discontinuities in S and use the differential dS to denote them (the differential operator needs to be distinguished from the time derivative, which can jump up without there being a discontinuity in the level). Now $dM = \beta dS - \alpha d\dot{S}$. But there has not been a step change in money supply ($dM = 0$), so there would need to be a step depreciation by the amount

$$dS = \frac{1}{\beta}\left(dM + \alpha d\dot{S}\right) = \frac{\alpha\mu}{\beta^2}.$$

But a step change in the exchange rate would mean riskless supernormal profits (at a potentially infinite rate), since with perfect foresight each investor would know that the exchange rate would jump at $\overline{T}$. Consequently, each would want to attack before $\overline{T}$ was reached, and R would go to zero before $\overline{T}$.

In fact, it is clear that with perfect foresight the exchange rate cannot jump at all, and this "no arbitrage" condition pins down the attack time, z. What has to happen, instead, is that the jump down in the money supply at the point of attack (due to the fall in reserves) just offsets the new anticipated rate of depreciation of the (now floating) currency. Thus,

$$dM = dR,$$
$$dS = \frac{1}{\beta}\left(dR + \frac{\alpha\mu}{\beta}\right),$$

so

$$dR = -\frac{\alpha\mu}{\beta}.$$

As a result, the currency crisis unfolds as follows (depicted in Figure 1.1): at z, speculators trade in part of their money holdings for foreign exchange, reducing reserves to zero and shifting down money holdings so that they equal $D(t)$. The money supply at this point starts growing at rate μ, while at the same time the exchange rate starts floating, depreciating at rate μ/β.

Let us consider the instant before the abandonment of the peg (when it has not yet been attacked). At this point

$$R(z^-) = R(0) - \mu z.$$

We need the remaining reserves to be completely exhausted by the attack,

$$R(0) - \mu z = \frac{\alpha\mu}{\beta}.$$

so

$$z = \frac{1}{\mu}\left[R(0) - \frac{\alpha\mu}{\beta}\right]. \tag{1.7}$$

This equation determines the point at which the attack occurs, and is successful (see Figure 1.1).

1.3. The Shadow Exchange Rate

Flood and Garber (1994) present a more intuitive version of the first-generation model that involves comparing the exchange rate peg to its value if the currency were floating — the shadow exchange rate $\widetilde{S}$. Start with the fundamental equation (1.6), which applies to a floating exchange rate, and calculate its value as if reserves were zero and money were simply equal to domestic credit, $\widetilde{M}(t) = D(t)$. From Equation (1.6),

$$\dot{\widetilde{S}} = \frac{1}{\alpha}\left(\beta\widetilde{S} - \widetilde{M}\right). \tag{1.8}$$

We find a solution to this differential equation by the method of undetermined coefficients. We postulate a solution

$$\widetilde{S}(t) = \lambda_0 + \lambda_1\widetilde{M}(t),$$

where λ_0, λ_1 are coefficients whose values are to be determined. Substituting the trial solution into (1.8), noting that $\widetilde{M} = \mu$,

$$\lambda_1 \mu = \frac{1}{\alpha} \left[\beta \left(\lambda_0 + \lambda_1 \widetilde{M}(t) \right) - \widetilde{M}(t) \right].$$

Grouping terms,

$$\widetilde{M}(t) = (\beta\lambda_0 - \alpha\mu\lambda_1) + \beta\lambda_1 \widetilde{M}(t).$$

For our trial solution to make sense, we need left-hand and right-hand sides to be equal for any value for $M(t)$, so

$$\beta\lambda_0 - \alpha\mu\lambda_1 = 0,$$
$$\beta\lambda_1 = 1,$$

implying that

$$\lambda_0 = \frac{\alpha\mu}{\beta^2},$$
$$\lambda_1 = \frac{1}{\beta}.$$

The following equation thus describes the evolution of the shadow exchange rate:

$$\widetilde{S}(t) = \frac{\alpha\mu}{\beta^2} + \frac{1}{\beta}\widetilde{M}(t). \tag{1.9}$$

Since $\dot{M} = \mu$, from (1.9) $\dot{\widetilde{S}} = \frac{\mu}{\beta}$, and is identical to $\dot{S}$ when floating prevails. The two curves meet at the point $(z, \overline{S})$ — see Figure 1.2. If $\widetilde{S}(t)$ is more **appreciated** than actual (pegged) exchange rate $S(t)$ (i.e., below it), then there is no crisis. When it crosses the exchange rate peg, then the crisis occurs, and the exchange rate reverts to the floating rate $S(t)$.

1.4. Applications

There have been numerous applications of first-generation models. Blanco and Garber (1986) look at credit growth in Mexico

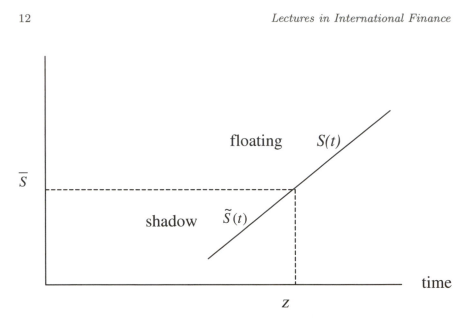

Figure 1.2.   Shadow exchange rate.

and conclude that a first-generation model explains the 1982 crisis. Flood and Garber (1994) also apply first-generation models, to other crashes, e.g., tulip bubbles and German hyperinflation in the 1920s. Komulainen (2004) extends first-generation models and applies them to emerging markets.

1.5.   Caveats and Extensions

The first-generation currency crisis model is elegant in its simplicity, and has the advantage of making clear predictions concerning the causes of crises and their timing. Like all models, it focusses on particular aspects of reality to the exclusion of others. However, as we will see below that more recent currency crises do not square very well with its predictions, and some of its assumptions are clearly unrealistic and at variance with other macro-financial models. Some of the more serious limitations are the following:

- Obviously, the assumption of perfect foresight is a problem, because it rules out the very thing we see in an exchange rate crisis, namely a step devaluation. This can be fixed by introducing uncertainty in the form of additive shocks and assuming no **expected** profit opportunity (Flood and Garber, 1994, appendix). Krugman (1979) also allows for uncertainty about reserve levels. More complicated models introduce asymmetric information. Broner (forthcoming) shows that when there are informed and uninformed investors, attacks may not be triggered when the shadow exchange rate reaches the parity; instead, the timing of a crisis becomes more uncertain, and there may be several possible equilibria. Asymmetry in information is discussed more extensively in the next chapter.

- Krugman's original article allowed for sticky domestic prices (not flexible prices as above). This makes the dynamics more complicated and makes it hard to calculate the attack time analytically, but is more realistic. Often, currency crises are associated with real exchange rate overvaluation (leading to trade deficits) — ruled out by the assumption of PPP.

- It may not be the case that governments choose to float when reserves run out. Other post-collapse regimes are possible, e.g., a new peg, faster credit creation, etc. The latter has been studied by Obstfeld (1984), and introduces the possibility of multiple equilibria.

- UIP is not empirically verified. More realistic models include a risk premium, and Flood and Marion (2000) make the risk premium depend on a perceived volatility measure. Conjectures about volatility can be self-fulfilling in this model.

- Finally, and this leads us to second-generation models, government behaviour is mechanistic in first-generation models because it does not involve any optimisation. If the authorities react to speculators' actions, and themselves act strategically, this produces a much more complicated and rich model. In some crises, the level of reserves has seemed less important in triggering a devaluation than other variables that directly affect utility. The decision to defend or not generally reflects wider macroeconomic conditions, in particular the level of unemployment (or output) and inflation. Sole focus on the existing stock of reserves is also misplaced in the case of financially developed economies. Countries with access to capital markets can borrow funds in order to intervene, and they can intervene in forward and derivative markets without directly using reserves. In addition, they have other instruments with which to defend their currency — principally the level of interest rates. Given the range of instruments available, it is best to consider a devaluation or float as at least in part a voluntary decision, rather than the inevitable consequence of the depletion of reserves.

Chapter 2

Second-Generation Currency Crisis Models

2.1. Background

The first-generation models were inspired by a particular set of historical events, and the same was true of the second-generation models. The crises in the European Monetary System (EMS) in 1992–1993 did not fit the predictions of first-generation models. The EMS was created in 1979 to limit fluctuations around central parities for currencies in the Exchange Rate Mechanism (ERM). Though designed to be a symmetrical system, in practice the strongest currency, the deutsche mark, became its centre, and starting in 1981 there were frequent downward realignments of the other currencies against the deutsche mark (Chart 2.1). In this period, countries like France were subject to faster monetary growth and higher inflation; pressures on their reserves led to periodic realignments, often after a brief speculative attack.

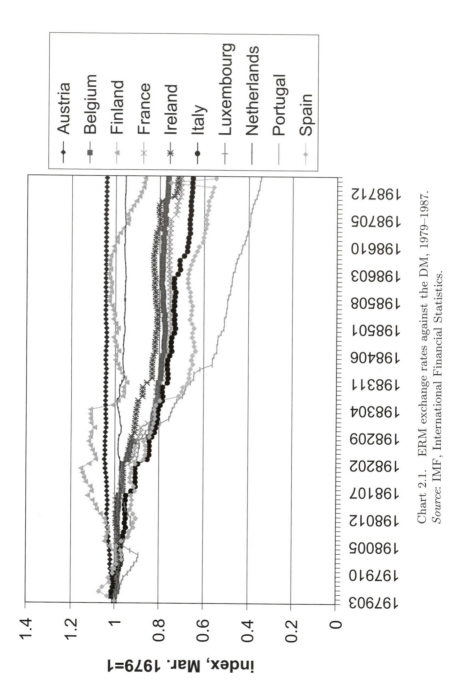

Chart 2.1.   ERM exchange rates against the DM, 1979–1987.
Source: IMF, International Financial Statistics.

By 1987, however, the situation had changed as inflation rates had dropped considerably; monetary discipline had been adopted by most ERM countries. From 1987 to September 1992 there were no more realignments. Moreover, the signing of the Maastricht Treaty with its plan for monetary union among at least a subset of the EMS countries led to anticipations of further exchange rate stability.

However, exchange rate crises in 1992–1993 shattered that rosy outlook. In September 1992, speculative attacks led both the pound sterling and Italian lira to drop out of the ERM. Further attacks on the French franc and other currencies led early in August 1993 to an abandonment of the narrow bands of fluctuation (plus or minus 2.25 percent from central parities) and adoption of bands of plus or minus 15 percent. Thus, speculative attacks had essentially succeeded in destroying the system. See Box 2.1 for a description of the unfolding of the EMS crisis.

Box 2.1. Timeline of the Crisis in the EMS, 1992–1993

1992

- June 2. Danish voters reject the Maastricht Treaty on Economic and Monetary Union.
- August. Pound sterling falls to a new low against the deutsche mark, despite record intervention, and Italian lira falls below ERM floor.
- September 13. Lira is devalued by 7 percent. Bundesbank lowers interest rates.
- September 16. Heavy intervention by the Bank of England and increase in the minimum lending rate fail to stem speculative pressure. The UK government announces withdrawal of sterling from the ERM.
- September 17. The lira's participation in ERM is suspended. Spanish peseta is devalued by 5 percent within the ERM. French franc falls to its ERM floor.
- September 21. France narrowly approves the Maastricht Treaty, and French franc again approaches ERM floor.

(Continued)

Box 2.1. (*Continued*)

1993

- January 30. Irish pound devalued by 10 percent within the ERM.
- January to February. Continued pressure on the franc.
- April to May. Bundesbank lowers interest rates; French election of a pro-European government led by Edouard Balladur and an easing of speculative pressures on the franc permit the Bank of France to lower interest rates.
- May to June. French interest rates briefly go below those in Germany, leading the French finance minister to speculate that the franc might take over ERM leadership from the deutsche mark. Cool reception from Germany leads to a renewal of speculation against the franc.
- July 29. Bundesbank does not lower discount rate as expected. Massive speculative flows against all other currencies in favour of the deutsche mark result.
- August 2. After an emergency weekend meeting of finance ministers and central bank governors, currency fluctuation bands are widened from plus or minus 2.25 percent to 15 percent.

Sources: IMF (1993) and Jeanne and Masson (1996).

From the perspective of first-generation models, the economic fundamentals did not justify many of those speculative attacks, nor did their timing seem linked to potential exhaustion of reserves (except in the case of the pound sterling, which was subjected to a well-publicised attempt by George Soros to break the Bank of England, which led Britain to abandon its peg). Some governments whose currencies were attacked (e.g., France, Denmark) did not have large deficits or rapid monetary expansion, nor was there any evidence of an overvalued exchange rate. Tellingly, two years after the crisis their exchange rates (and also Belgium's) were back close to their (unchanged) central parities (Chart 2.2). The pound sterling (now floating) also returned to its previous ERM parity of 3.94 DM.

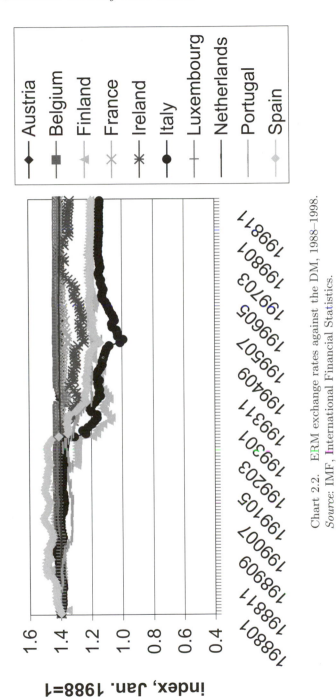

Chart 2.2. ERM exchange rates against the DM, 1988–1998.
Source: IMF, International Financial Statistics.

Another unexplained feature was that the timing of the 1992–1993 crises seemed to be dictated not by economic forces but rather by political events such as the prospects for ratification of the Maastricht Treaty in France or public disagreements between French and German finance ministers. While these events could certainly serve as triggers for changes in economic fundamentals, as argued (though with some difficulty) by advocates of first-generation models, they were also consistent with shifts in expectations that were purely self-fulfilling. If so, they might be completely unrelated to past or future economic fundamentals.

The economic environment facing countries in a world of high capital mobility was at variance with what was assumed by first-generation models. By 1990, and consistent with EMS commitments, EU countries had mostly eliminated capital controls, increasing the possibility of cross-border capital flows. With high capital mobility, speculators can more easily take a position against a particular currency, but, in addition, a government can borrow reserves to defend it so that exhaustion of a country's own reserves need not trigger a crisis or preclude further exchange market intervention. Moreover, the monetary authorities have other instruments to defend the currency, in particular raising interest rates. Attention must be paid not just to the ability of the authorities to defend their currency, but also to their willingness to do so. To be relevant, currency crisis models have to endogenise their behaviour. The tool for doing so is the Barro–Gordon model, which effectively summarises the key features of the economy highlighted in second-generation currency crisis models.

2.2.   The Barro–Gordon Model

This model, which dates back to 1983 (Barro and Gordon, 1983), has been influential in analysing monetary policy in closed and open economies; it will constitute a key building block in the remaining chapters on currency crises, policy coordination, and currency unions. It is a barebones model of output determination that nevertheless combines two crucial features: **nominal rigidities** (of wages and prices) and **time consistency issues** relating to policy announcements or commitments.

Nominal rigidities are a crucial feature of models of monetary transmission. With perfect flexibility of wages and prices, there is no role for monetary policy in affecting output or other real variables. In the presence of nominal rigidities, in contrast, the central bank can affect real magnitudes and there is scope for active use of monetary policy to offset shocks or moderate business cycles. In the Barro–Gordon model, nominal rigidity is introduced because private sector expectations are formed (and, presumably, wage or price contracts signed) before the monetary policy setting for the period is known. Monetary policy is not known because a shock to output is not yet observed when those expectations are formed. When the central bank observes the shock, it sets money growth optimally to respond to that shock. In the simplest version of the model, it optimises a quadratic objective function of output and inflation with respect to just the current period.

Time consistency issues arise because the central bank has an informational advantage (and acts after expectations are formed and after observing the shock) and also because the central bank wants to stimulate output. It takes the private sector's expectations as given when it sets its policy. It is in the central bank's interest to influence expectations, perhaps by announcing that it will not generate inflation. The first-best policy would involve a precommitment by the central bank that it will use monetary policy only to offset shocks, not to generate systematic inflation. However, in these models, there is an incentive for the central bank to ignore its commitment and to generate inflation anyway. We will see why below.

2.2.1. *A closed economy version*

The central equation concerns the linkage between **monetary surprises** and output growth. Because contracts are signed before policy is decided, the predicted part of money growth (m) has no effect on output (y) — just the excess of money growth over its expected value (denoted by a superscript ^{e}):

$$y = \bar{y} + \gamma(m - m^e) - u. \tag{2.1}$$

The reason why there is a positive effect ($\gamma > 0$ by assumption) is that by raising prices beyond what was expected, or lowering interest rates, the central bank produces greater demand for individuals' labour and firms' output. However, the precise transmission mechanism is not made explicit. The variable u is an output shock, which, if positive, lowers output. This sign is convenient in deriving effects but is arbitrary. $\bar{y}$ is the natural rate of output growth — the value that would prevail in the absence of shocks or monetary surprises. It is conventionally assumed to be constant.

Monetary policy is guided by an objective function that weighs together the losses from deviating from targets for output and inflation. The first-best value for inflation (in the absence of shocks) is assumed to be zero (though it could just as easily be some value, like 2 percent, that corresponds more closely to what central banks actually target, because of biases in actual inflation statistics and a concern to avoid deflation). As for output, another crucial assumption is that the central bank targets a value y^* that is above its natural rate $\bar{y}$. This may be the case because there is some distortion in labour or product markets (due to monopoly power or insider behaviour), which keeps output suboptimally low. Again, this is not made explicit, however. So the authorities' objective function is:

$$L = (y - y^*)^2 + \theta\pi^2. \tag{2.2}$$

The parameter θ captures the relative importance of inflation versus output deviations. In the simplest version of the model, inflation is simply equal to money growth:

$$\pi = m.$$

Thus, money growth can simply be replaced by inflation in (2.1), and the central bank can be assumed to set that variable directly.

It is important to be clear about the sequence of events in the model. First, the private sector's expectations are formed; then, a shock u is observed; and finally, the central bank chooses money growth to minimise (2.2). To solve the model, we work backward. The private sector knows that the central bank minimises its objective function, so it can solve for that optimal policy, conditional on some (unobserved) value of u and taking as given expectations m^e. The first-order condition (FOC) of that minimisation is

$$\frac{\partial L}{\partial m} = 2\gamma[\bar{y} + \gamma(m - m^e) - u - y^*] + 2\theta m = 0.$$

This yields the optimal policy

$$m = \frac{1}{\gamma^2 + \theta} \left\{ \gamma^2 m^e + \gamma u + \gamma(y^* - \bar{y}) \right\}. \tag{2.3}$$

The central bank's optimal policy has three parts. The first term within { } brackets indicates that it partially **accommodates expectations**: inflation that is expected but does not occur constitutes a negative monetary surprise which will lower output. However, accommodation is not complete, because there is a cost to inflation being above zero. The second term is the **optimal response to the shock**: the central bank provides monetary stimulus to offset (again partially) its impact. Finally, the last term captures a structural **bias towards positive inflation** that results from the labour/product market distortion mentioned above: $k \equiv y^* - \bar{y}$ is a measure of the size of this distortion.

Private agents can use (2.3) to calculate the expected value for money growth, and equate it to the value m^e. In particular, take expectations of (2.3) and set $E(m) = m^e$. Solving for m^e yields the following (after noting that $E(u) = 0$):

$$m^e = \frac{\gamma k}{\theta}.$$

If $k = 0$, then monetary growth is expected to be zero — its first-best value. However, a positive distortion $(k > 0)$ creates an incentive for the central bank to inflate; this incentive is rationally built into the private sector's expectations, and therefore the central bank accommodates it. In equilibrium, therefore, the central bank's reaction function [substituting out for expectations in (2.3)] is given by

$$m = \frac{\gamma k}{\theta} + \frac{\gamma}{\gamma^2 + \theta} u. \tag{2.4}$$

It is important to note that with **effective precommitment** the central bank would attain a lower value for the loss function (2.2). In this case, the central bank could maximise while taking expectations m^e as being under its control [but still equal to $E(m)$]. Thus, it could announce a policy rule $m = \overline{m} + \beta u$, where $\overline{m}$ is chosen to maximise expected utility. Substituting the rule into L and maximising with respect to $\overline{m}$ yields $\overline{m} = 0$. The optimal response to a shock, derived by maximising with respect to β, would be as before. Thus, the first-best policy would set $m = \gamma u/(\gamma^2 + \theta)$, yielding zero inflation on average (since shocks u have mean zero). In this case, the central bank would want to precommit to zero expected inflation, that is, not to attempt to correct the distortion k, since $m^e = 0$ would give the lowest loss. However, precommitment is assumed not to be possible.

2.2.2.   *The open economy*

To be useful for our purposes, the model needs to be adapted to a world with two or more interdependent economies. This requires modifications to the output equation and/or to inflation determination. We will study several variants in the chapters that follow.

The simplest modification involves noting that the exchange rate is closely linked to the inflation rate and to monetary growth. Thus, in some second-generation currency crisis models, the rate of inflation is simply replaced by the rate of change of the exchange rate. Moreover, the policy choice of the authorities is narrowed down to a choice of whether to keep the exchange rate fixed (and maintain the currency peg) or to allow it to change, with the authorities abandoning the fixed rate regime.

More generally, however, both output and inflation may be affected by monetary growth in the rest of the world. For instance, we can alter the output supply equation to include monetary surprises in the rest of the world, as follows:

$$y = \bar{y} + \gamma(m - m^e) + \mu(m^* - m^{*e}) - u, \tag{2.5}$$

where a star indicates the foreign variable. The issue of the sign of the monetary transmission μ then arises. Structural models give a number of channels by which monetary expansion abroad would affect domestic activity. In this context, the nature of the exchange rate regime is important. Under a freely floating exchange rate regime, like other asset prices the exchange rate is likely to be more flexible than goods prices. Thus, monetary expansion abroad would be expected to produce a depreciation of that country's nominal exchange rate in excess of the rise of domestic prices, yielding a real depreciation. That real depreciation abroad (which is a real appreciation for the home country) would reduce output in the home country, *ceteris paribus*, as the country's exports became more expensive, so $\mu < 0$. Under fixed exchange rates, the nominal depreciation would not occur, but instead there might be some upward pressure on prices abroad — producing real appreciation, not depreciation, and $\mu > 0$. Thus, the real exchange rate channel alone would suggest positive transmission of monetary surprises on output under fixed rates but negative transmission under floating rates.

However, there is another channel. Monetary expansion abroad would lead to a rise in economic activity in the foreign economy, and the income effect would tend to increase the home country's exports — positive transmission, even under flexible exchange rates. The net effect of relative prices and activity is ambiguous under floating rates. However, empirical multicountry models suggest that the second effect could dominate if the foreign country is large and open, like the United States, leading to positive transmission [see Helliwell and Padmore (1985)]. In contrast, if the foreign country and the home country compete in third markets but have little direct trade, the real exchange rate effect would dominate since there would be only a small activity effect. The following table summarises the expected transmission effects of monetary policy on output.

	Weak activity effects	Strong activity effects
Fixed exchange rate	Positive transmission	Positive transmission
Floating exchange rate	Negative transmission	Positive transmission

In some models (most appropriate for an exchange rate regime with some fixity of the exchange rate), the rate of inflation may also be linked to foreign as well as domestic monetary policy. For instance, if one writes

$$\pi = \alpha m + (1 - \alpha)m^*,$$

then inflation is equal to a weighted average of money growth at home and abroad, with weights summing to one so that the relationship is homogeneous — a doubling of world money growth doubles domestic inflation. The home central bank may choose whether to offset fully or partially the effect of foreign monetary policy. In general, if output were also affected, as in (2.5), it would not be optimal simply to offset completely the effect on inflation of foreign monetary policy. In this case, there would be scope for welfare-improving policy coordination between the home and foreign central banks.

2.3. An Influential Second-Generation Model

Getting back to currency crises, we now study a model with endogenous policy that is built on the Barro–Gordon model. This model is the first of those presented in Obstfeld (1996)[1]; a second model, based on government debt, is also presented in that paper. A more intuitive account with extensive discussion of the EMS crises is given in Obstfeld (1994).

2.3.1. *Key assumptions*

- The authorities maximise an objective function, devaluing (floating) or not depending on which policy yields greater utility.
- There is a distortion that leads the central bank to want to stimulate activity by loosening monetary policy.
- Central banks cannot credibly precommit to carry out the first-best policy, because that policy is not time consistent.
- The private sector acts first, formulating inflation expectations, then the central bank observes the shock to output and decides exchange rate policy.
- Monetary policy controls the inflation rate directly, and inflation is equated with the rate of depreciation, $\pi = \varepsilon$. There is no consideration of foreign monetary policy.

2.3.2. *The model*

The government (or central bank) minimises

$$L = (y - y^*)^2 + \beta\varepsilon^2 + C(\varepsilon), \tag{2.6}$$

where y^* is the central bank's target for output, $\varepsilon = s - s_{-1}$ is the rate of depreciation (if positive), and $C(\varepsilon)$ is a realignment cost that is paid if ε is non-zero.

---

[1]See also Sarno and Taylor (2002).

An expectation-augmented Phillips curve explains the level of output:

$$y = \overline{y} + \alpha(\varepsilon - \varepsilon^e) - u, \tag{2.7}$$

where $\overline{y}$ is the natural rate of output, and ε^e are price/wage setters' expectations of devaluation (before observing the supply shock u or the actual level of ε). It is assumed that $k \equiv y^* - \overline{y} > 0$ so that there are dynamic inconsistency problems which the government cannot solve because it cannot precommit.

In the absence of realignment costs [i.e., $C(\varepsilon) \equiv 0$], the central bank would want to respond actively to any shock that arose, and the optimal policy would give

$$\varepsilon = \frac{\alpha(k + u) + \alpha^2 \varepsilon^e}{\alpha^2 + \beta}, \tag{2.8}$$

yielding the following value for the loss function

$$L^{\text{flex}} = \frac{\beta(k + u + \alpha\varepsilon^e)^2}{\alpha^2 + \beta}, \tag{2.9}$$

which is obviously less than the loss function value when the exchange rate is constrained to be fixed ($\varepsilon \equiv 0$):

$$L^{\text{fix}} = (k + u + \alpha\varepsilon^e)^2, \tag{2.10}$$

since $\beta/(\alpha^2 + \beta) < 1$, except for the special case $u = -k - \alpha\varepsilon^e$, when they are equal.

However, with costs of realigning (i.e., $C > 0$), fixed rates will be optimal for values of u in some interval. Let

$$C(0) = 0,$$
$$C(\varepsilon|\varepsilon > 0) = \overline{c} > 0, \tag{2.11}$$
$$C(\varepsilon|\varepsilon < 0) = \underline{c} > 0,$$

and define the interval $\underline{u} < u < \overline{u}$, where fixed rates are preferred over floating. The intuition is that only for sufficiently large (positive or negative) shocks would the central bank want to pay fixed realignment costs (either depreciating when there are negative supply shocks, $u > \bar{u}$, or appreciating for large positive shocks, $u < \underline{u}$). These limits are defined by a comparison of (2.9) and (2.10), yielding

$$\bar{u} = \frac{1}{\alpha}\sqrt{\bar{c}(\alpha^2 + \beta)} - (k + \alpha\varepsilon^e) > 0,$$

$$\underline{u} = -\frac{1}{\alpha}\sqrt{\underline{c}(\alpha^2 + \beta)} - (k + \alpha\varepsilon^e) < 0.$$

Given the private sector's expectations, the rational expectation of ε is

$$E(\varepsilon) = E(\varepsilon|u < \underline{u})\Pr(u < \underline{u}) + E(\varepsilon|u > \bar{u})\Pr(u > \bar{u}), \qquad (2.12)$$

where the two terms are expected revaluation and devaluation, respectively. Note that the probability associated with u being in the interval (and fixing being optimal) is multiplied by a value of zero for ε, so it does not appear in (2.12).

Obstfeld goes on to assume that the shock u is uniformly distributed in the interval $[-\mu, \mu]$, which allows direct computation of the probabilities. The probability density is drawn in Figure 2.1 on the assumption that the upper and lower shock thresholds are within the support of the distribution.

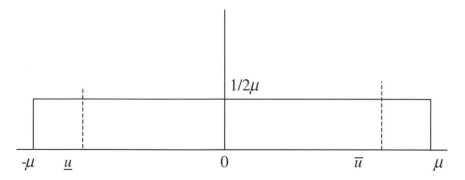

Figure 2.1. Distribution of shocks to output.

Now it is obvious from the diagram that with this distribution

$$\Pr(u < \underline{u}) = \frac{\mu + \underline{u}}{2\mu},$$

$$\Pr(u > \overline{u}) = \frac{\mu - \overline{u}}{2\mu},$$

and

$$E(u|u < \underline{u}) = \frac{\underline{u} - \mu}{2},$$

$$E(u|u > \overline{u}) = \frac{\overline{u} + \mu}{2},$$

so

$$E\varepsilon = \frac{\alpha}{\alpha^2 + \beta} \left[\left(1 - \frac{\overline{u} - \underline{u}}{2\mu} \right) (k + \alpha\varepsilon^e) - \frac{\overline{u}^2 - \underline{u}^2}{4\mu} \right]. \qquad (2.13)$$

In equilibrium $E\varepsilon = \varepsilon^e$, so we need to find a fixed point of (2.13). This is plotted as the upper segment of Figure 2.2. However, there are two other segments that correspond to cases where the limits $\overline{u}$ and $\underline{u}$ are no longer interior points of the uniform distribution. There can be as many as three intersections of the 45° line in $(\varepsilon^e, E\varepsilon)$ space, corresponding to the fixed points.

Figure 2.2 illustrates how the slope and position of the curve (2.13) over its various segments determine the number of intersections. If the slope is always less than one, then after the first intersection (the lowest rate of depreciation), the curve stays below the 45° line, so there is only intersection. There will thus be only one fixed point and no possibility of multiple equilibria.

The existence of three intersections is more likely if the devaluation cost $\overline{c}$ is low, the slope α of the Phillips curve is high, inflation aversion β is low, and the credibility distortion k is big. In this case, the temptation is great to use a devaluation to stimulate output. Reducing the distortion or increasing the weight on inflation will shift the curve in the figure to the right, producing in the limit only one equilibrium with a value of $E\varepsilon$ close to zero. So **the key message is** not that crises are always the result of self-fulfilling expectation, but

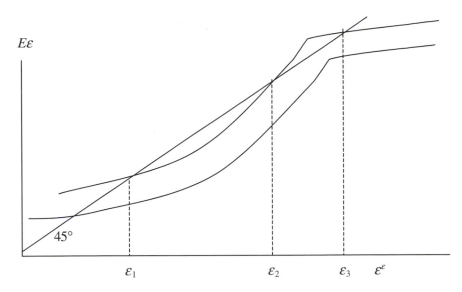

Figure 2.2. Fixed points for exchange rate expectations.

that only in certain ranges are multiple equilibria possible.
If economic fundamentals are very good, there are no crises, while
if they are very bad, crises are inevitable. In the middle, there are
"sunspot equilibria", so named because the model does not specify
which equilibrium would be chosen. Instead, the choice is assumed
to be determined by extraneous variables, "sunspots".

The intuition given to the figures is the following: if for some
reasons investors expect a high depreciation rate, then it will be
likely to occur. Thus, expectations are partially self-fulfilling. This is
true because higher expectations of inflation/devaluation make the
trade-off worse for the government: if the latter does not validate
them, then output will be lower [Equation (2.7)], lowering welfare.
However, crises are not certain even in this case, since they also
depend on a bad realisation of the output shock.

An important criticism of these models (see below) is that we
do not have a theory for why investors would coordinate on one or
another of the three equilibria.

2.4.   A More General Second-Generation Model

Jeanne (1997) shows that there is no need to assume a uniform distribution in order to get analytical results, and that in general there will be self-fulfilling expectations if only mild restrictions are imposed on the distributions of shocks. Moreover, the government's utility function and the private sector's behaviour can be specified in a very general way. This canonical model can thus be usefully applied in a variety of contexts.

Policymakers are assumed to be of two types: "tough" policymakers defend at all costs, while "soft" ones defend only if the net benefit is positive. Policymakers are soft with probability μ (having $\mu < 1$ is not crucial for the theoretical model, but it helps to fit the data).

The net benefit at t (B_t) of maintaining the peg can be decomposed into two parts. One of them depends on the private sector's assessment at $t - 1$ of the probability of a devaluation (opt out) by the policymaker at t (π_{t-1}), while the other one (b_t) is assumed to be independent of it:

$$B_t = b_t - \alpha\pi_{t-1}. \tag{2.14}$$

Let

$$\phi_t \equiv E_t b_{t+1},$$
$$u_{t+1} \equiv b_{t+1} - \phi_t.$$

The variable ϕ_t denotes the **economic fundamentals** within this model. Note that the formulation does not exclude the possibility that the fundamentals could be generated by some autoregressive process and hence could be partially predictable. It is simply assumed that innovations u to the fundamentals are independently and identically distributed and have a density function $f(.)$ that is continuous, symmetric, and strictly increasing in $(-\infty, 0)$—hence strictly decreasing in $(0, \infty)$.

An equilibrium is a fixed point in the reciprocal mapping between the beliefs of investors and policymakers' actions. Because of the rationality of expectations, the devaluation probabilities must equal the objective probability that the government is soft and that the net benefit is negative:

$$\pi_t = \mu \Pr[B_{t+1} < 0] = \mu \Pr[u_{t+1} < \alpha \pi_t - \phi_t] = \mu F[\alpha \pi_t - \phi_t],$$
$$(2.15)$$

where $F(.)$ is the cumulative distribution function of $f(.)$.

Equation (2.15) is the central equation of the model. It shows that ϕ_t summarises all the exogenous state variables that matter, justifying the term "fundamentals".

Since both sides of (2.15) are increasing with π_t, it may have multiple solutions so that a given level of the fundamentals can be consistent with several levels of the devaluation probability.

Jeanne goes on to derive under what conditions multiplicity arises:

Proposition 1. *If $\mu \alpha f(0) < 1$, the devaluation probability is uniquely determined by (and strictly increasing in) the fundamental ϕ_t.*

Proposition 2. *If $\mu \alpha f(0) > 1$, there are two critical values of the fundamentals such that: if $\phi > \overline{\phi}$ or $\phi < \underline{\phi}$, the devaluation probability π_t is uniquely determined by (and strictly decreasing with) the fundamental ϕ_t and if $\underline{\phi} < \phi < \overline{\phi}$ the devaluation probability π_t may take three values.*

Some intuition behind the conditions can be obtained from the plot of the cumulative distribution (Figure 2.3). A necessary condition for that curve to cross the $45°$ line twice (since the leftmost intersection is from above) is that it must have a slope greater than unity at some point. Since f takes its maximum at zero, Proposition (1) follows. Whether the curve crosses the $45°$ line also depends on the position of the cumulative distribution, which is shifted up or down

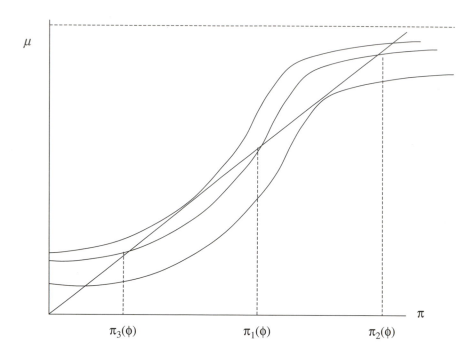

Figure 2.3.   Plot of equilibria for probability of devaluation.

by the economic fundamentals. If the fundamentals are very good, the cumulative distribution only intersects once, at a low probability of devaluation; if very bad, there is also one intersection, at a high devaluation probability. The points of tangency of the distribution functions with the 45° line in Figure 2.3 define the intermediate range of fundamentals $\underline{\phi} < \phi < \overline{\phi}$, where multiple equilibria are possible.

2.5.   Empirical Applications

There have been many analyses and formal tests of the first- and second-generation models. For instance, Eichengreen *et al.* (1995) found some evidence that crises seem to have arbitrary elements, not related to economic fundamentals; thus they conclude that crises may reflect self-fulfilling expectations.

Cole and Kehoe (1996) specify a dynamic general equilibrium model, where sunspot equilibria are possible when investors have to choose whether or not to roll over their short-term lending to the government. If they expect a crisis, they can provoke one by refusing to lend, because then the government has liquidity problems. They conclude that the model when calibrated to Mexico in 1994–1995, is useful for understanding the debt/devaluation crisis there. They suggest that shifts between equilibria may have occurred as a result of political events, e.g., the Colosio assassination in March 1994, the resignation of the attorney general, etc. In their model, the maturity of the debt has a big influence on the possibility of devaluation. Only short debt maturity opens the door to crises — though why the government allowed maturities to get so short is unexplained. Presumably they did so because investors would not allow longer maturities (or not lend at reasonable rates). An alternative approach to modelling the crisis empirically is to focus on the authorities' credibility, as in Agénor and Masson (1999), drawing on Drazen and Masson (1994). This approach does not produce multiple equilibria but rather a gradual deterioration of investors' sentiment as they discover the authorities' true objectives.

Jeanne (1997) uses French data for the ERM in 1992–1993, and he finds that macroeconomic fundamentals are not sufficient to explain speculative attacks on the franc. Jeanne and Masson (2000) test a dynamic version of the Markov-switching model and reject the alternative that there is a single regime and no sunspots. In this dynamic model, rather than being limited to three, rational-expectation equilibria are potentially infinite in number.

Masson (1999a, 1999b) shows that several Asian countries affected by crises were in a range where multiple equilibria were possible, using a modified version of the model Jeanne (1997) applied to France. The fundamentals here are the trade balance and the initial level of debt. Provided the trade surplus is not large enough to repay existing debt and if the debt is not rolled over, then a crisis can occur. While not a formal test for jumps between equilibria, the paper quantifies the range in which sunspot equilibria can occur and observes that several of the crisis countries were in this range, based on data for end-1996.

2.6.   Critique of Models with Multiple Equilibria

Critics of models with multiple equilibria object to them because typically no theory is provided of what leads investors to coordinate on one or another of the possible equilibria. Hence, the model adds a level of indeterminacy. It is further argued that the assumption of common knowledge of the economic fundamental is unrealistic. Morris and Shin (1998, 2002) show that removing that assumption, instead adding a small amount of uncertainty about the fundamentals in a context in which each investor observes a private signal, eliminates multiple equilibria if investors know how other investors will act and apply a sophisticated reasoning concerning their behaviour.

2.6.1.   *The Morris and Shin model*

Assumptions

The following assumptions are key to their model:

- There is no common knowledge of the fundamentals: each agent has a private signal of the fundamental that contains a "small" amount of uncertainty.
- Agents know how the other agents behave.

The gist of the argument is as follows [taken from Pesenti (2001)]. Assume two speculators, each deciding whether to attack or not on the basis of what the other agent is expected to do (since each alone cannot exhaust reserves and provoke a currency devaluation, but together they can). The following table gives the pay-off matrix in case each attacks (A) or does not attack (N). Doing nothing (not attacking) has no costs or return, but mounting an attack has a cost of 1 and, if successful, a return of X.

Agent II

		A	N
Agent I	A	$X-1, X-1$	$-1, 0$
	N	$0, -1$	$0, 0$

Common knowledge

This framework can be used to justify multiple equilibria when X is known [see Obstfeld (1996)]. If the pay-off (inversely related to the fundamental) from a successful attack is sufficiently low $(X < 1)$, neither attacks. If $X > 1$, then there are two Nash equilibria, an attack and a no-attack equilibrium, provided [as in Obstfeld (1996)] X is a variable (possibly random) that is known to both agents. This is so because the best response to an attack by the other agent is to attack oneself, while the best response to a non-attack is not to attack.

Absence of common knowledge

However, assume instead that X is not observed exactly by both agents. Each receives a private signal Z which is distributed symmetrically around the true value of X. Assume that the true value is bounded by $Z - \delta < X < Z + \delta$, where δ is some (small) positive number; Z is the best estimate of X. Let P be the other agent's action; then each agent's expected pay-off from attacking is

$$\Pr[P = A] \cdot (Z - 1) + \Pr[P = N] \cdot (-1) = \Pr[P = A] \cdot Z - 1.$$

So $Z > 1$ is no longer sufficient to produce a positive expected profit relative to not attacking (whose pay-off is zero), because it is not certain that the other agent will attack. The other may not in fact have observed a large enough signal $\underline{Z}$ to justify an attack. On the contrary, if (say) agent I's signal $Z > 1$ is sufficiently close to 1 (by a margin that is much lower than δ), he/she will infer that the chance is close to 50 percent that II observed a signal $\underline{Z}$ less than 1 (since each agent's private signal is symmetrically distributed about the true value), and hence will not attack. The same argument applies to agent II (and is common knowledge); so by iterating this reasoning, an even larger signal will not justify attacking (since agent I will know that agent II will reason the same way). This will, in the limit, lead to a unique cut-off point $Z > Z'$ at which both agents will shift from a "no attack" to an "attack" equilibrium. Thus, multiple equilbria disappear. A more rigorous derivation with a continuum of agents is given in Morris and Shin (1998).

2.6.2. *Discussion*

This demonstration by Morris and Shin (2002) can however be criticised [done in comments by Atkeson and Rey and in Hellwig *et al.* (2005)]. First, a key assumption is that lack of common knowledge needs to be small. Is this empirically valid? Second, the information structure is not very general — it assumes that only the private signal is unknown, but that each agent knows how the other agent reasons. Thus there is uncertainty about the signal (the fundamentals) but not about the other agent's strategy in response to his own (private) signal. The latter is a very strong assumption that rules out all the interesting action in games such as poker. Third, the iterated elimination of dominated solutions, which is key to the derivation of a unique attack threshold, gives results that are in fact counter to the actual play of certain games in laboratory situations (Camerer, 1997). Fourth, multiple equilibria are common in other fields and result in general from models with non-linearities, so that the methodological preference of Morris and Shin for unique equilibrium models seems hard to justify. Fifth, in many cases, models with a unique equilibrium are unable to account for the volatility in financial markets, and jumps between equilibria are a way of introducing that volatility (Masson, 2001b). Finally, Hellwig *et al.* (2005) show that the Morris and Shin abstracts from the role interest rates play in aggregating information. If such a role is allowed for, multiple equilibria are robust to a lack of common knowledge. For all of these reasons, it does not seem desirable *a priori* to rule out currency crisis models with multiple equilibria. However, the Morris and Shin focus on asymmetry of information has led to interesting further research on speculative attack models of both first and second generation.

Chapter 3

Currency Crises and Contagion in Asia

3.1. The Shock of the Asian Crises of 1997–1998

Like Latin America and Europe before it, East Asia faced in 1997–1998 a severe crisis that led to an abandonment of currency pegs and brought with it large declines in output and a drying up of capital inflows. While most of the "emerging market" countries (Thailand, Malaysia, Singapore, Korea, and Taiwan) in Asia did not have rigid currency pegs (though Hong Kong had a currency board with a fixed peg to the US dollar), they had all to a greater or lesser extent exhibited extended periods of stability of their exchange rates vis-à-vis the dollar, leading to an implicit commitment to a narrow range of values for their currencies. Chart 3.1 depicts the pre-crisis exchange rate paths against the dollar for Indonesia, Korea, Malaysia, and Thailand. While the first two countries' currencies exhibited steady,

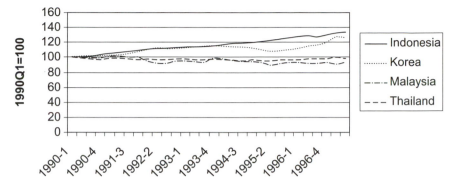

Chart 3.1. Exchange rates of selected Asian countries, 1990–1997Q2.
Source: IMF, International Financial Statistics.

though moderate, depreciation, the latter two resembled officially fixed rates. The monetary authorities in those countries in fact operated policy in such a way as to peg the rate, and when Thailand started running current account deficits the central bank sold foreign exchange reserves to maintain the implicit peg. Reserve outflows continued as doubts about the peg's sustainability mounted, and the authorities also intervened in the forward market in a desperate attempt to turn things around. When this did not work they abandoned the peg at the beginning of July 1997. The Thai baht quickly depreciated, and also the currencies of neighbouring countries. The crisis spread to Korea and Hong Kong in the latter part of the year. Despite large-scale lending by the International Monetary Fund, exchange rates (except those of Hong Kong, which maintained its currency board, and China, which because of capital controls was largely unscathed by the crisis) depreciated precipitously — especially that of Indonesia (Chart 3.2). The depreciations were accompanied by corporate and financial bankruptcies, large output declines, and severe economic disruption.

Again, events had unfolded in an unexpected way, leading to a reconsideration of the adequacy of crisis models and development of a new generation. In Asia, there was a sharp contrast in the image

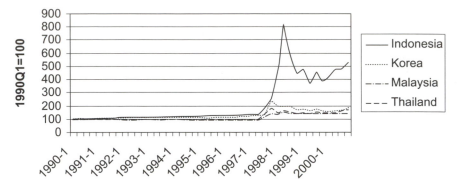

Chart 3.2. Exchange rates of selected Asian countries, 1990–2000.
Source: IMF, International Financial Statistics.

of the countries concerned, before and after the crisis — from Asian "miracle" to "mirage", as their success was called into question (Box 3.1). Most of the economies affected had been fast growing with few fiscal problems or unemployment; indeed, it was common to refer to them as "Asian tigers". Inflation was low, close to levels in North America or Europe, and hence did not pose a threat to a fixed exchange rate. Moreover, unlike the European economies that had suffered the 1992–1993 EMS crisis, unemployment did not make it difficult for the Asian economies to accept the constraints of a fixed exchange rate. Instead, it was clear that problems in domestic financial sectors and perverse incentives to borrow short-term in foreign currencies made these countries very vulnerable to shocks.

Box. 3.1. The Asian Financial Crises, 1997–1998

Countries in East Asia in 1996 to early 1997 had few of the macroeconomic symptoms of fragile economies. Growth remained high, consistently above 5 percent per year, and for a number of them, over 7 percent; inflation remained contained well under 10 percent; and current account deficits, though widening, were less than 5 percent (Singapore and Taiwan were in fact in surplus). The exception was Thailand,

(Continued)

Box 3.1. (*Continued*)

which suffered from overheating of the economy (this was also true to a lesser extent of Malaysia) as evidenced by a large current account deficit, almost 8 percent of GDP — in excess of Mexico's deficit of 6 percent of GDP at the time of the tequila crisis. The crisis in Thailand was in fact largely anticipated, as evidenced by a trend decline in the stock market and persistent capital outflows. When the decline in reserves made further intervention to preserve the value of the Thai baht difficult, the authorities allowed a devaluation of the implicit peg on July 2, 1997.

Despite an IMF program with Thailand augmented by Japanese and other financing, the Thai crisis quickly led to a snowballing decline of the baht and downward pressures on the currencies of Indonesia, Malaysia, the Philippines, and Singapore. For a few months, the spread of the crisis seemed to be limited to those countries. However, in October, Taiwan devalued, and Hong Kong and Korea came under sharp speculative pressure. The crisis was especially severe in Indonesia, leading to an extended depression, but all the countries in the region suffered sharp economic slowdowns, widespread unemployment, and in many cases corporate and financial bankruptcies.

The countries affected had very different characteristics. Hong Kong had a strong official peg to the dollar that embodied an automatic response of monetary conditions to the balance of payments; it had large fiscal and current account surpluses. Indonesia and Korea had already embraced a degree of exchange rate flexibility so did not have de facto or official pegs like the others. Korea was an economic powerhouse, a member of the OECD; Singapore was an enormously successful country with a strong balance of payments and large foreign exchange reserves.

Nevertheless, there were some features that most of these economies had in common, which helped to explain why the problems of Thailand were so severe, and why other economies in the region were also viewed as vulnerable, despite strong macroeconomic fundamentals.

(*Continued*)

Box 3.1. (*Continued*)

They can be summarised as follows [see for instance Alba *et al.* (1999) and Eichengreen (1999)]:

- Large capital inflows had sown the seeds of future problems because their domestic effects were resisted with high interest rates, which accentuated the incentives on banks and non-financial companies to borrow abroad in foreign currencies, usually non-hedged and short-term. This led to currency and maturity mismatches, which vastly amplified the severity of currency depreciations, once they occurred.
- Financial sector weaknesses — implicit public guarantees for bank lending and poor lending practices — were pervasive, due in part to inappropriate financial sector liberalisation and ineffective regulation. Countries like Thailand and Korea perversely maintained restrictions on foreign direct investment (generally considered to be stabilising) while liberalising volatile short-term borrowing abroad (an example was the creation of the Bangkok International Banking Facility). The result was excessive and risky foreign borrowing and domestic lending.
- Poor governance on the part of corporates and their close relationship with governments ("crony capitalism") with the expectations of bailouts, combined with the failure of foreign lenders to properly assess risks, also contributed to excessive borrowing and lending.
- The exchange rate was an important part of the story; the stability of currency values against the dollar encouraged taking on unhedged foreign currency exposure, and it also shackled monetary policy. Sterilising inflows led to a perverse increase in domestic interest rates, which encouraged further foreign borrowing. The capital account surpluses meant current account deficits, widening vulnerability.
- The resulting build-up of stocks of short-term foreign liabilities far in excess of foreign exchange reserves meant that governments were

(*Continued*)

Box 3.1. (*Continued*)

unable to resist the effect on their economies of a shift in sentiment of international investors.

Subsequent to the crises, East Asian countries have attempted to remedy the problems identified above, by improving financial regulation and corporate governance, limiting foreign currency and maturity mismatches, adopting greater exchange rate flexibility, and accumulating much larger foreign exchange reserves.

There were several causes for the deterioration of the region's current account balance, which triggered the crisis. The electronics industry, which contributed much to the region's exports, had undergone a downturn. The yen had depreciated sharply against the dollar, so that countries whose currency was linked to the dollar (most of the other East Asian countries) were suffering losses of competitiveness relative to Japan. And China had itself earlier decided to devalue, tending to make it more competitive relative to the other Asian economies.

Whatever the trigger, it was the virulence of the crisis and its further spread to other countries that surprised. The magnitude of the output decline was related to widespread financial sector problems, which spilled over into the non-financial sector. Financial intermediaries (and corporations) had borrowed in foreign currency, taking advantage of lower interest rates (and disincentives to borrow on domestic financial markets). To some extent this was the result of financial liberalisation that was incomplete and embodied perverse incentives (for instance, no reserve requirements on banks' foreign borrowing). Thailand had created the Bangkok International Borrowing Facility explicitly to encourage foreign borrowing by Thai companies. There were also moral hazard problems because of close connections between financial institutions and politicians. For instance, state-owned banks may have expected government bailouts if things went bad so that they did not worry about the creditworthiness of borrowers. Even private banks were often examples of "crony capitalism" because of links between their owners and politicians in power, and ownership links with companies that borrowed from the banks. Banks took excessive risks hoping to profit handsomely but not bear the costs if outcomes were unfavourable.

However, even healthy countries suffered attacks, including Singapore and Hong Kong. Though the attack on Hong Kong's currency board was ultimately unsuccessful, it continued for months, and to beat it back, the Hong Kong Monetary Authority adopted drastic measures, including purchasing a large portfolio of local stocks in order to squeeze speculators.

In the countries that did experience a depreciation, there were severe balance sheet problems as the domestic currency value of foreign debts increased dramatically, making debt service impossible and forcing widespread bankruptcies of both the corporate borrowers and the banks that had lent to them. Thus, the crisis highlighted the dangers of balance sheet effects from foreign borrowing and the perverse incentives to borrow abroad (unhedged) — features that were not present in then-existing currency crisis models. Third-generation models added these features to an open-economy macro framework, in order to better understand the nature of crisis propagation and contagion.

3.2.   A Third-Generation Model

An example of such a model, which highlights the role of balance sheet effects, is given in an article by Aghion *et al.* (2001). While having some of the same properties as second-generation models, in particular the possibility of self-fulfilling crises, the way expectations feed back on the devaluation probability is different here. The focus is not so much on government actions as on the lending behaviour of financial institutions and on credit constraints.

3.2.1. *Key assumptions*

- Purchasing power parity (PPP) holds *ex ante*, but not *ex post*, as a shock to the exchange rate has real effects and causes a deviation from PPP. Shocks include a shift in expectations. There is a shock only in period 1; thereafter, the economy converges towards a non-stochastic steady state.
- Prices are sticky so that a shock to PPP causes the nominal exchange rate to move.
- Credit markets are imperfect: firms are credit constrained and can only borrow a fixed multiple of their current real wealth, or cash flow. Moreover, they are limited in the amount of domestic currency borrowing, forcing them to borrow abroad.
- Interest parity holds, and money market equilibrium takes a standard form.
- The central bank targets the interest rate from period 2 onward, but not in period 1.
- Production is given by a standard production function, but the size of the capital stock depends on the amount of borrowing, i.e., capital is best thought of as "working capital".

3.2.2. *Equations of the model*

Interest parity:

$$1 + i_t = (1 + i^*)\frac{S_{t+1}^e}{S_t},$$

where, as before, i is the domestic interest rate, i^* the foreign rate, and S is the nominal exchange rate.

Money market equilibrium relates the nominal money supply M^s to money demand which is proportional to the price level P, while real money demand depends on real output y and the nominal interest rate:

$$M_t^s = P_t \cdot m^d(y_t, i_t).$$

The above two equations yield the IPLM curve which links the period 1 exchange rate with period 2 output (it is assumed that the central bank follows an interest rate target from period 2 onward, and expected PPP holds so that $P_2 = S_2^e = S_2$):

$$S_1 = \frac{1 + i^*}{1 + i_1} \frac{M_2^s}{m^d(y_2, i_2)}. \tag{IPLM}$$

This is a negative relationship between S_1 and y_2. On the right-hand side of this equation, i_1 is endogenous (for given M_1^s and predetermined P_1), while i_2 is given by monetary policy.

Entrepreneurs can at most borrow an amount d proportional to their cash flow w:

$$d_t \leq \mu w_t,$$

and the amount of domestic currency debt is limited to $d_t^c \leq d_t$. This assumption is motivated by the crisis countries, which had limited domestic financial markets and incentives for foreign borrowing, as firms did not take into account the potential for crisis. Working capital is the only input to production and it fully depreciates within one period, so that capital is given by

$$k_t = w_t + d_t,$$

and if the credit constraint is binding, the production function can be written as

$$y_t = f\left((1 + \mu)w_t\right).$$

Assuming that a proportion α of entrepreneurs' profits is consumed or distributed, then output can be written (in period 2) as

$$y_2 = f\left((1 + \mu)(1 - \alpha)\left\{y_1 - (1 + r_0)d_1^c - (1 + i^*)\frac{S_1}{P_1}(d_1 - d_1^c)\right\}\right), \tag{W}$$

where r_0 is the real rate on borrowing. This also gives a negative relationship between S_1 and y_2, the W curve.

Short-run equilibrium is given by the intersection of the IPLM and W curves. This can produce one or two stable equilibria in (S_1, y_2) space. Note that the W curve has a vertical segment along the S_1 axis: for values of the exchange rate above (i.e., more depreciated than) some critical value, output is zero. Figure 3.1 shows the case where there is only one equilibrium with high output, while Figure 3.2 illustrates a unique equilibrium with low (zero) output, where currency depreciation drives profits to zero and Figure 3.3 shows three intersections (only two of which are stable — the right and left ones). The rightmost corresponds to an appreciated exchange rate and high output. However, if there are expectations of a large currency depreciation, consumers reduce their money demand because expected output is lower. Reduced money demand will lead to a depreciated currency, which in turn reduces profits and hence output, leading to the left-hand equilibrium with zero output.

As in second-generation models, a currency crisis does not occur independently of the fundamentals. A negative productivity shock (shifting the f function) or a tightening of credit constraints (lower μ) would shift the W curve down and might move the economy from

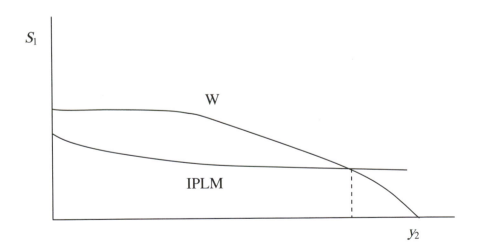

Figure 3.1.   Unique good equilibrium.

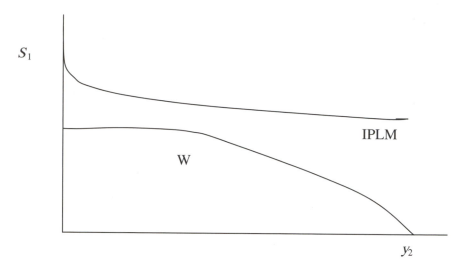

Figure 3.2.   Unique bad equilibrium.

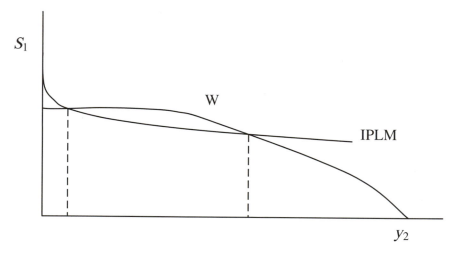

Figure 3.3.   Multiple equilibria.

the case depicted in Figure 3.1 to that in Figure 3.3. This could in turn trigger a crisis if expectations shifted at the same time.

However, the central bank can influence the possibility of multiple equilibria. By tightening monetary policy, it shifts down [not up, as is stated in Aghion *et al.* (2001, p. 1131)] the IPLM curve — starting, say, from the case in Figure 3.3, and possibly reverting to the case of Figure 3.1.

A necessary [not sufficient, despite what is stated in Aghion *et al.* (2001, p. 1133)] condition for multiple equilibria is that the W curve intersect the vertical axis below the point where the IPLM meets it. This condition can as be written as

$$\frac{y_1 - (1 + r_0)d_1^c}{(1 + i^*)(d_1 - d_1^c)} < \frac{1 + i^*}{1 + i_1}\frac{M_2^s}{P_1}\frac{1}{m^d(0, i_2)}.$$

3.2.3. *Notes on third-generation models*

Multiple equilibria in this model are not due to endogenous government behaviour but rather due to the interaction between private agents. They produce the self-fulfilling expectations through balance sheet effects on output. However, not all third-generation models have multiple equilibria.

In this model, by extension, it is natural to see the joint occurrence of currency crises and banking crises (since banks, even if not explicit in this model, would suffer the same balance sheet effects in a more complicated model with financial intermediaries).

Furthermore, this model directs attention at moral hazard and information asymmetries that may produce more foreign currency borrowing than is desirable from society's standpoint.

There is an indirect link between future fiscal deficits and crises today, because governments are typically drawn into bailing out their financial systems. But this is a very different channel from the first-generation one, in which there is a known and continual expansion of domestic credit. Here, fiscal policy problems are not the trigger for the financial crises; they are the consequence of them. Nevertheless, Aghion *et al.* show that their model can be extended to include first- and second-generation features.

The model formulated in Aghion *et al.* (2001) has certain unappealing features. First, credit multipliers are an ad hoc mechanism that require a deeper analysis, for instance, in order to understand the difference between countries at different stages of financial development. Second, the treatment of capital is inadequate; assuming it all depreciates in one period produces dramatic and unrealistic effects on output. Third, in the model, output is solely driven by investment; including some intertemporal consumption demand would dampen fluctuations. Finally, the model, though ostensibly multiperiod, incorporates assumptions concerning the nature of shocks and the stance of policy that essentially reduce it to a one period context.

3.2.4. *Policy conclusions*

A model similar to that of Aghion *et al.* led Paul Krugman to draw the following policy conclusions, in "Analytical Afterthoughts on the Asian Crisis" — see his website.

- Monetary policy should resist currency depreciation in order to minimise the extent of balance sheet problems so that the criticism that was often made of this aspect of IMF packages — i.e., tight money — was not justified.
- However, the IMF focus on fiscal austerity exacerbated the downward pressure on output.
- Financial support by the IMF could in principle help to allow servicing of a country's foreign currency debts but in fact IMF resources were too small to make much of a difference. More effective was the coercion exerted on foreign lenders to maintain their exposure, in the case of Korea.
- Emphasising structural problems (crony capitalism) and attempting to restructure financial sectors worsened the crisis of confidence and was a major mistake on the part of the international institutions called to provide assistance.
- Capital controls should be considered in such cases, to prevent the crisis from having a snowballing effect on the exchange rate, and from producing widespread bankruptcies. This was the course

followed by Premier Mahathir in Malaysia, and it is generally considered to have moderated the damage from the crisis. Aghion *et al.* (2004) show that the model implies that economies with an intermediate level of financial development are more vulnerable to currency crises and that therefore they should be careful with capital account liberalisation.

3.3. Contagion Effects

3.3.1. *Background*

A striking feature of the Asian crises was the spillover from the initially impacted country, Thailand, to most of its neighbours. The extent of the spillover was new, but the phenomenon was not. To some extent, each of the post-1970 crises has exhibited contagion effects, including the Bretton Woods crisis of 1971–1973, and the third world debt crisis in the early 1980s. Not surprisingly, the EMS crisis of 1992–1993 exhibited contagion since it was the whole system that was under attack. However, contagion seemed more difficult to explain in Latin America at the time of the "tequila crisis" (Mexico, 1994–1995) when countries like Argentina and Brazil with few similarities or linkages with Mexico suffered from attacks, and was especially difficult to understand in the case of the Asian crisis.

A vast literature has developed that attempts to explain the reasons for contagion. However, the word "contagion" has been used in many different senses by various authors. It is necessary, at a minimum, to distinguish between "interdependence" and "contagion". Countries are linked together by trade and financial linkages; there are spillovers that explain why events in one country (including a financial crisis) would have effects in another country (especially one that is a close neighbour or for other reasons maintains close ties). Normally, we expect these spillovers to be positive — so that economic expansion in one country produces expansion in its neighbours, but this is not true in all models or for all shocks. Conversely, a crisis in one country would deteriorate the financial situation of others.

A three-legged taxonomy relative to contagion is proposed by Masson (1999a, 1999b). In particular, we can distinguish between **monsoonal effects**, events caused by the global environment facing developing countries (which includes such things as the world oil price or the stance of US monetary policy); **spillovers** that operate through the conventional trade and capital flow linkages between developing countries; and **pure contagion**, that is, a crisis triggered by a shift in expectations in one country that occurs at the same time as a shift in another country, for instance, because there are jumps between equilibria due to correlated sunspots or informational linkages. A model illustrating these channels is developed below, taken from Masson (1999a).

This taxonomy is not universally accepted. Those who question the relevance of jumps between multiple equilibria (see Morris and Shin, 2002) would also dispute their role in contagion. Moreover, the emphasis of third-generation models on financial linkages has led some to concentrate on "financial contagion", which abstracts from macroeconomic linkages.

3.3.2. *A currency crisis model with contagion*

Masson (1999a) develops the channels for monsoonal effects, spillovers, and correlated jumps between multiple equilibria in the context of a hybrid currency crisis model that could be considered of the first generation since a devaluation is triggered by reserve losses. The exchange rate enters the trade equation for the home country, and thus is a channel for spillovers, while monsoonal effects are captured by the level of world interest rates. Because the level of interest rates paid by developing country borrowers depends on the probability of a crisis, expectations of the latter can be self-fulfilling. Higher borrowing costs make it more likely that reserves will fall below the threshold level, triggering a crisis. Moreover, expectations of a crisis in a foreign country will increase expectations of a crisis in the home country.

The model, stripped to its bare essentials, is based not on money market equilibrium but on the current account of the balance of payments. The home country (we will consider the symmetric case of a second emerging market country shortly) faces net export receipts T which are stochastic, while it inherits outstanding debt D on which it must pay a market-determined interest rate. The latter is equal to the world riskless rate (say on US treasuries), i^*, which is exogenous, plus compensation for expected depreciation or default, depending on whether the foreign borrowing is in domestic currency or in foreign currency (the two versions are isomorphic). Depreciation or default is assumed to be in amount δ and to occur with probability π, so that a risk neutral investor would set the domestic interest rate i at

$$i = i^* + \pi\delta$$

so as to equalise the expected returns on emerging market debt with that from holding US treasury securities.

Provided that existing debt is rolled over (at the new prevailing interest rate), the balance of payments, that is, the change in reserves, equals

$$R_{+1} - R = T_{+1} - iD.$$

A devaluation next period is triggered if the level of reserves R_{+1} reaches zero, and this will be true if

$$R + T_{+1} - iD \leq 0.$$

Note that when expectations are formed, the trade balance next period is not known — it is stochastic, but investors are assumed to know the distribution of shocks to it and to use this knowledge in forming devaluation expectations. The assumption of rationality enforces equality of those expectations with the objective probability:

$$\pi = \Pr[R + T_{+1} - iD \le 0] = \Pr[R + T_{+1} - (i^* + \pi\delta)D \le 0]. \quad (3.1)$$

As before, both sides of the equation depend positively on the probability, and multiple equilibria may thus exist. Putting it in the form of Jeanne's model (1997) allows one to apply his necessary and sufficient conditions for multiple equilibria (see Chapter 2). Let

$$b_{+1} \equiv R + T_{+1} - i^* D,$$
$$\alpha \equiv \delta D.$$

Then, as in Jeanne's model, we denote the fundamental ϕ by

$$\phi \equiv Eb_{+1} = R + ET_{+1} - i^* D,$$

and its innovation ε by

$$\varepsilon \equiv b_{+1} - \phi.$$

Then the model becomes

$$\pi = \Pr[\varepsilon \le \alpha\pi - \phi].$$

We assume that the shocks ε have cumulative distribution function F so that

$$\pi = F[\alpha\pi - \phi].$$

Conditions on slope and tangency given in Jeanne's model thus determine whether we are in a single or multiple equilibrium region. In particular, by increasing α a higher level of outstanding debt makes the cumulative distribution steeper in terms of π and helps to satisfy a necessary condition for multiple equilibria. The fundamentals are more likely to be in the multiple equilibrium region if initial reserves are not too high nor net exports too large.

The scope for contagion can be introduced by adding another emerging market borrower. However, now their trade balances are linked because a devaluation by one worsens the net exports of the other. It is assumed for simplicity that a devaluation by each worsens the other's trade balance by Δ if the latter does not devalue relative to T_{+1}. If a devaluation has already occurred by this period, then this will shift down T_{+1} as well. We introduce superscripts a and b to distinguish the two countries.

Now the probability of devaluation next period by country a is equal to

$$\pi^a = \Pr[R_{+1}^a \leq 0] = (1 - \pi^b) \Pr[R^a + T_{+1}^a - i^a D^a \leq 0]$$
$$+ \pi^b \Pr[R^a + T_{+1}^a - \Delta - i^a D^a \leq 0], \qquad (3.2)$$

and similarly for country b:

$$\pi^b = (1 - \pi^a) \Pr[R^b + T_{+1}^b - i^b D^b \leq 0] + \pi^a \Pr[R^b + T_{+1}^b - \Delta - i^b D^b \leq 0]. \qquad (3.3)$$

These two equations illustrate the monsoonal effects, spillovers, and jumps between multiple equilibria as channels for linking a crisis in one country to a crisis in another. Monsoonal effects, that is, the effect of global economic conditions, operate through the value of i^* : higher global interest rates will make both countries more likely to run into difficulties servicing their debts. Spillover effects operate through the trade competitiveness effects that may have already occurred: a devaluation by b will have lowered the starting position for T_{+1}^a. Finally, there may be a linkage in expectations, either because devaluation in one country, if it occurred next period, would make it more likely that the second country would also devalue, or, if multiple equilibria are possible, simply because jumps between multiple equilibria are correlated, i.e., correlated sunspots. The latter two explanations are related, because the expected spillover effects may shift the solution of each of the equations from one with a unique equilibrium to one with multiple equilibria. The possibilities are discussed in Masson (1999a) and illustrated numerically.

Alternatively, one may try to find psychological or financial reasons why expectations may shift in the same direction. Some possible explanations are given in the next subsection.

3.3.3.   *Other channels for contagion*

- **Common lenders.** If a large bank, for instance, suffers losses from its loans to one emerging market borrower, it may be forced to liquidate its portfolio in other markets. Why should this affect other emerging market lenders only (and not their holdings of advanced country claims)? There may be portfolios dedicated to holding emerging market assets from a certain area (regional funds), and also the need to de-leverage as a result of a crisis will exacerbate the liquidation, provoking a "flight to quality" and a shift out of riskier, developing country bonds. But it needs to be understood that there is an implicit assumption of market failure: other investors are for some reason unwilling to step in and purchase assets which are (by assumption) mis-priced.
- **Wake-up call.** According to this hypothesis, a crisis in Thailand showed investors that there were problems in all Asian countries ("crony capitalism" or similar shaky financial systems) — explaining regional contagion. A similar story could be made about Mexico and Latin America. But why did investors take so long to wake up to problems which were always there, and why did they go back to sleep again so soon after the crises (so that spreads two years after Mexico's 1994–1995 crisis were at all-time lows)?
- **Linkages through the international financial system.** As the IMF loaned more and more of its finite resources to Asian countries, the likelihood of being able to bail out further countries declined, increasing their vulnerability. This story would be more convincing if IMF bailouts were shown to be effective in stopping crises.
- **Political contagion.** An unsuccessful defence of a parity in one country may lower the political will in others, either because they

are linked in a common effort that is put in danger (e.g., the EMS) or because popular support for sacrifices is weakened.

3.3.4. *Empirical work*

The set of empirical articles on contagion is too vast to be surveyed here, but various conference volumes [for instance, Agénor *et al.* (1999) and Glick *et al.* (2001)] provide a sampling. Evidence of "contagion" seemed to be strongest in the Asian crisis, and also that evidence suggested that contagion mainly affected countries in the same region rather than in other regions. There has been much less evidence of high correlations between various emerging market countries during later crises, though the Russian crisis had worldwide repercussions. Forbes and Rigobon (2002) in their empirical work conclude "No Contagion, Only Interdependence", noting that it is important to understand that increased apparent correlation in crisis periods may simply be due to greater variance.

3.3.5. *Herding models*

Herding among investors is a related phenomenon that it is argued, characterises the behaviour of international investors. Banerjee (1992), and Bikchandani *et al.* (1992) show why it may be rational for investors to ignore their private signals and imitate others, in a context of imprecise knowledge of fundamentals. Banerjee, for instance, cites as example the choice by 100 diners whether to go to restaurant A or B, which are side by side. Even if everyone shares the idea that A is likely to be better than B, they also observe the choices of others and give some weight to the latter. If the person who chooses first gets a signal that A is better, his action to eat at that restaurant may override the private signals of the remaining diners that B is better, leading everyone to eat at A, even though the latter is in fact inferior.

Herding models help provide a story for coordinating on one of several equilibria. However, the assumptions made are quite specific, namely sequential play and observing the actions of others. It is said that the big hedge funds were imitated by others at the time of the Asian crises, but this situation may not generally apply to the international financial system. Herding in any case is not the same thing as contagion: though it can explain why an influential investor like George Soros might induce others to short the Thai baht, it would not explain why all of them would also short the Malaysian ringgit.

Part II

International Economic Policy Coordination

Chapter 4

Is Policy Coordination Desirable?

4.1. Interdependence

Interactions between governments acting independently can give sub-optimal outcomes because of the spillover effects of a country's policy on other countries. If each government attempts to maximise its own objective function, using only its own instrument(s) and taking other countries' policies as given, the result is a Nash equilibrium. Hamada (1976) showed that under a system of pegged exchange rates with a fixed quantity of reserves (such as the gold exchange standard) in which each country had to run restrictive demand policies in order to defend its peg, the Nash equilibrium would be Pareto inferior to joint maximisation of utility (that is, coordination), because in the latter regime, countries need not contract demand to the same extent. Gains to coordination could accrue under floating exchange rates as well; for instance, Oudiz and Sachs (1984) argued that the

1979–1980 oil price shock induced too restrictive monetary policies, because countries did not internalise the efforts of other countries to lower inflation.

The high point of international macroeconomic policy coordination was the late 1970s to mid-1980s, associated with the 1978 Bonn Summit, the 1985 Plaza Agreement, and the 1987 Louvre Accord (see Box 4.1 for a chronology). While the Bonn Summit involved agreement on a variety of policies, including European fiscal expansion and US energy conservation policies, the latter two episodes were principally aimed at achieving an orderly decline in the value of the US dollar.

Box 4.1. A Selective Chronology of Post-World-War-II International Economic Policy Coordination

- 1944. Meeting at Bretton Woods, New Hampshire, establishes the International Monetary Fund and World Bank and creates the "Bretton Woods regime" of fixed but adjustable exchange rates.
- Late 1940s and 1950s. US Marshall Plan aid for European reconstruction is channelled through Organization for European Economic Cooperation (later called the OECD), which also is instrumental in lowering intra-European trade barriers and coordinating macroeconomic policies.
- 1952. European Coal and Steel Community is formed.
- 1956. Treaty of Rome is signed by Belgium, France, Italy, Luxembourg, the Netherlands, and West Germany, establishing the European Economic Community.
- 1971. The Smithsonian Agreement attempts to salvage the Bretton Woods regime by revaluing other major currencies against the dollar; the attempt fails to stem balance of payments pressures, and in March 1973 generalised floating of exchange rates begins amid speculative outflows from the US currency.

(Continued)

Box 4.1. (*Continued*)

- 1973. "Library Group" of finance ministers of the United States, France, West Germany, and the United Kingdom meets, and later in the year G-5 coordination (now including Japan) begins.

- 1978. Bonn Summit of heads of state and government of the G-7 (G-5 plus Canada and Italy) agrees to a package of measures that includes US energy policy changes reducing oil imports, fiscal expansion in West Germany and Japan, and a commitment to proceed with trade liberalisation negotiations.

- 1979. The European Monetary System (EMS) is formed, establishing central parities and bands of fluctuation around member-country exchange rates in order to limit their volatility.

- 1985. Plaza Agreement by G-5 finance ministers and central bankers is designed to bring about an orderly depreciation of the US dollar, which is widely viewed as overvalued and has already begun to decline from its peak. Agreement leads to substantial coordinated intervention in foreign exchange markets.

- 1987. Louvre Accord indicates intention of major powers to stabilise the dollar after its decline, and reiterates the need for expansionary fiscal policies in Japan and Germany and for fiscal discipline in the United States.

- 1991. Maastricht Treaty setting out the path to Economic and Monetary Union in Europe is signed.

- 1993. Agreement is reached to widen EMS bands of fluctuation to plus or minus 15 percent in order to save the system in the face of speculative attacks that led to withdrawal of Italy and the United Kingdom from the exchange rate mechanism and several devaluations of other currencies against the deutsche mark.

- 1995. The World Trade Organization (WTO) is established, taking over responsibility for facilitating trade liberalisation from the General Agreement on Tariffs and Trade. The WTO also includes dispute settlement mechanisms.

(Continued)

Box 4.1. (*Continued*)

- 1999. The euro is launched, replacing the currencies of 11 European Union countries, and the European Central Bank is established.
- 2004. The European Union expands to 25 countries with the admission of 10 new members from central and eastern Europe.
  Sources: Ghosh and Masson (1994, Appendix) and Meyer *et al.* (2002, Appendix B).

The literature on policy coordination initially focussed on gains from using one instrument in each country — usually monetary policy — either set independently or as a result of joint optimisation. In the usual terminology, this involves a comparison of the Nash equilibrium and the Cooperative equilibrium. A key issue is the nature of spillovers between countries, as detailed in Canzoneri and Henderson (1991). In the case where countries are identical and face the same shock, whether the Nash equilibrium uses the policy instrument too actively or not enough (when compared to the Cooperative equilibrium) depends critically on whether monetary expansion is transmitted positively or negatively to other countries. It also depends on the sign of the shock. If shocks are different in sign or magnitude, or countries respond differently to shocks and to economic policies, then it is very difficult to get any general theoretical results.

More recent models consider coordination of two policy instruments, monetary and fiscal policies. Much of this work has its roots in the European Monetary Union, where monetary policy is centralised in the European Central Bank and fiscal policies (coordinated or not) are decentralised and remain under the control of national governments. We will consider some of the relevant models in Chapters 6 and 7 when we discuss currency unions.

The models developed in this chapter and next — based on the Barro–Gordon model described in Chapter 2 — are simple one- or two-period models. The inclusion of more than one period (or a gap between the formation of expectations and the authorities' policy choices) introduces the concept of time inconsistency into policy choice. The absence of a mechanism to precommit to the optimal policy limits the set of policies to time consistent ones, that is, those on which the government will not have an incentive to default after uncertainty has been resolved. Policy coordination in multi-period models is treated in Buiter and Marston (1984) and a number of later contributions.

Much of the literature on policy coordination assumes that we know the correct model of the real world (and its parameters) — clearly an unrealistic assumption. In the next chapter, we will briefly explore the effect of parameter uncertainty on optimal policies and potential gains from coordination.

There are a number of good surveys of the literature on policy coordination. They include Persson and Tabellini (1995), McKibbin (1997), Drazen (2000, Section 12.5), and Meyer *et al.* (2002). A non-technical survey is Horne and Masson (1988).

4.2. A Simple Model of Monetary Policy Coordination

As in the standard Barro–Gordon model, each government ($i = 1, 2$) minimises a loss function that depends on output (y) and the rate of inflation (π):

$$L_i = y_i^2 + \theta \pi_i^2. \tag{4.1}$$

Assume that the target for output is the natural rate (so there is no distortion k that would lead to incentives to generate surprise inflation), and define y such that it is deviation from the natural rate. This is the first term in (4.1). The target for inflation is also zero. These two variables are assumed to be determined by money growth at home (m_i) and abroad (m_j) as follows. Inflation is given by

$$\pi_i = \alpha m_i + (1 - \alpha)m_j, \tag{4.2}$$

where $j =$ the other country. In general, we would expect $0.5 \leq \alpha \leq 1$.

Output is determined by money growth surprises minus a shock u.

$$y_i = \gamma(m_i - m_i^e) - u. \tag{4.3}$$

The parameter γ is assumed to be positive. Note that each country is assumed here (but not in general) to have the same shock to its output, and that the latter is affected (positively) by monetary surprises in the home country only (this is relaxed later). Since each country has two targets and one instrument, it cannot attain its bliss point (i.e., where $y_i = 0$ and $\pi_i = 0$) independently of the other country. The reaction functions for each country optimising independently are given by differentiating the loss function, after substituting in for (4.2) and (4.3):

$$L_i = [\gamma(m_i - m_i^e) - u]^2 + \theta [\alpha m_i + (1 - \alpha)m_j]^2.$$

So

$$\frac{\partial L_i}{\partial m_i} = 2\gamma [\gamma(m_i - m_i^e) - u] + 2\theta\alpha [\alpha m_i + (1 - \alpha)m_j] = 0. \tag{4.4}$$

Since there is no distortion here and $Eu = 0$, the rationally expected value for money growth is $m_i^e = 0$.

If we solve (4.4), after eliminating expectations we can derive the reaction functions

$$m_i = \frac{1}{\theta\alpha^2 + \gamma^2} [\gamma u - \theta\alpha(1 - \alpha)m_j]. \tag{4.5}$$

Let us call the two reaction functions (for countries 1 and 2) $m_1 = \Pi^1(u, m_2)$ and $m_2 = \Pi^2(u, m_1)$ and plot them in (m_2, m_1) space. They are drawn as straight lines in Figure 4.1. Note first that both reaction functions are negatively sloped, and that Π^1 is flatter than Π^2 because each country's money supply affects its own variables more strongly than those abroad. However, in the general case the reaction functions can have positive slopes if spillovers take the

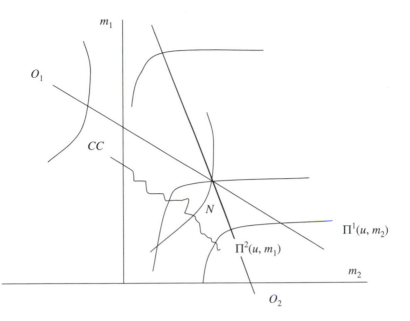

Figure 4.1.   Reaction functions and the Nash equilibrium.

opposite sign. Figure 4.1 plots the reaction functions for a negative
output shock $(u > 0)$.

The intersection of the two reaction functions yields the Nash
equilibrium (N), the result of each country taking the other's policy
as given and optimising with respect to its own instrument. Necessarily, neither country will reach its bliss point $(O_1$ and O_2, respectively),
since each has one instrument but two objectives.

Let us next examine how a country could get to its bliss point,
if it could use both instruments. Choosing country 1 in particular,
optimising with respect to its own and country 2's money growth
would yield two FOCs, Equation (4.4) plus

$$\frac{\partial L_1}{\partial m_2} = 2\theta(1 - \alpha)\left[\alpha m_1 + (1 - \alpha)m_2\right] = 0,$$

which yields

$$m_2 = -\frac{\alpha}{1 - \alpha}m_1. \tag{4.6}$$

Note here that country 1 would like country 2's money growth to have the opposite sign to its own. In the case of a negative output shock, country 1 wants to raise y by expanding its money supply, while it wants 2 to contract in order to offset the effects on inflation of its monetary expansion [by an amount that depends on the relative effects of the two moneys on 1's inflation — see Equation (4.6)].

Substituting (4.6) into (4.4) and solving, we see that at 1's bliss point

$$m_1 = m_1^e + u/\gamma,$$

and

$$m_2 = -\frac{\alpha}{1 - \alpha} \left[m_1^e + u/\gamma\right].$$

It can be verified that this yields $\pi_1 = 0$ and $y_1 = 0$, showing that with two instruments, and provided the effects of its policies are known, country 1 can neutralise inflation while keeping output at its natural rate.

In Figure 4.1, indifference curves radiate out from O_1 and O_2. For country 1 they are vertical where they intersect its reaction function, and for country 2, horizontal where they intersect its reaction function, because the respective FOCs set those derivatives to zero. Pareto efficiency implies that each country's welfare can only be increased at the expense of the other's, requiring the indifference curves to be tangent. It is obvious that at the Nash equilibrium N, the two countries' indifference curves cannot be tangent, hence the Nash is not Pareto efficient. The set of points that are Pareto superior to the Nash (i.e., where one or both country's welfare is higher than at N, but the welfare of neither is lower) is given by the lens bounded by the indifference curves for country 1 and country 2 that intersect at N. Pareto efficient points are given by points of tangency between the two sets of indifference curves. They constitute what is called the Contract Curve, and are depicted in the figure as CC. Policy coordination or cooperation yields a point on the contract curve that is in lens, hence is superior to the Nash equilibrium.

What does the cooperative solution look like? It will depend on the bargaining weights of the two countries, and it is useful to express the joint optimisation as a weighted sum of the two objective functions, using those bargaining weights. Let β be the weight of country 1. The cooperative solution would optimise with respect to both instruments

$$L = \beta L_1 + (1 - \beta)L_2.$$

Then the FOC are

$$\frac{\partial L}{\partial m_1} = \beta \left\{ 2\gamma \left[\gamma(m_1 - m_1^e) - u \right] + 2\theta\alpha \left[\alpha m_1 + (1 - \alpha)m_2 \right] \right\}$$
$$+ (1 - \beta) \left\{ 2\theta(1 - \alpha) \left[\alpha m_2 + (1 - \alpha)m_1 \right] \right\} = 0,$$

and

$$\frac{\partial L}{\partial m_2} = \beta \left\{ 2\theta(1 - \alpha) \left[\alpha m_1 + (1 - \alpha)m_2 \right] \right\}$$
$$+ (1 - \beta) \left\{ 2\gamma \left[\gamma(m_2 - m_2^e) - u \right] + 2\theta\alpha \left[\alpha m_2 + (1 - \alpha)m_1 \right] \right\}$$
$$= 0.$$

Note the symmetrical effect of the cross terms, that is, the effect of country i's instrument of country j's inflation (and vice versa), which will influence the optimal setting since it affects total welfare.

It is intuitively obvious and can be easily shown that if $\beta = 1$, we get to country 1's bliss point, and conversely for country 2 if $\beta = 0$. In general, however, the shock is not perfectly offset for either country.

Let us simplify further in order to compare the Nash and Cooperative solutions, denoted with N and C superscripts, respectively. Let us assume the two countries are identical in all respects and have the same weight in the joint objective function. In particular, we assume for now $\beta = 1/2$. Given this assumption, we know that under each regime the countries must adopt the same policies since they are identical in all respects. It is easy to show that the Nash equilibrium is given by

$$m^N = \frac{\gamma}{\gamma^2 + \alpha\theta}u,$$

for both countries while the cooperative solution is given by

$$m^C = \frac{\gamma}{\gamma^2 + \theta}u.$$

Since $\alpha < 1$, it is clear that $m^N > m^C$ if $u > 0$, that is, each country tries to expand to offset (still only partially) the negative output shock, while ignoring the effect on the other country's inflation, and this gives an over-expansionary policy outcome.

4.3.   Extensions

4.3.1.   *How to enforce the cooperative solution?*

It is important to understand that countries have incentives not to carry out an agreement to coordinate policies. The reaction functions that are the basis for the Nash equilibrium are precisely the best response in the face of a given policy by the other country, while those for the cooperative solution are not. So necessarily each country could do better if it thought that the other country would not retaliate in the face of its cheating on the policy bargain. Much has been written about trigger strategies to punish deviation, and reputational considerations would lead countries not to deviate from the cooperative solutions. The idea here is that even though cheating is profitable in the short run, it might preclude making welfare-enhancing bargains in the future. Also, institutions can be created with enforcement mechanisms, and choice of institutions has been modelled in a two-stage game. We will not discuss this here, but the next chapter will consider a special case in which fixed exchange rates substitute for joint optimisation and achieve the first-best solution.

4.3.2. *Cooperation can be welfare deteriorating*

If there is a distortion that leads countries operating independently to choose suboptimal (constrained) policies, cooperation may improve or worsen welfare. We show this by expanding the model above by assuming that the central bank's target for output is not the "natural rate" (see Chapter 2) and including an effect on output of the other country's monetary expansion, assumed to be transmitted positively. Positive transmission to country i would be consistent with fixed exchange rates and a real appreciation by country j. If country j expands its money supply faster than does country i, it depreciates i's real exchange rate, making that country more competitive, generating higher output in i.[1] So, instead of (4.3), we have

$$y_i = \gamma\left[(m_i - m_i^e) + \omega(m_j - m_i)\right] - u, \tag{4.7}$$

where $0 \le \omega \le 1$. Furthermore, we now assume that in each country the target for output growth is not zero (the natural rate) but some positive value k. Introducing this target creates an incentive to use monetary expansion to lower unemployment, even in the absence of shocks. This gives the following objective function:

$$L_i = (y_i - k)^2 + \theta\pi_i^2. \tag{4.8}$$

Now, the **Nash equilibrium** can be found by minimising (4.8), which yields

$$\frac{\partial L_i}{\partial m_i} = 2\gamma(1-\omega)\left\{\gamma\left[(-m_i^e + (1-\omega)m_i + \omega m_j\right] - u - k\right\}$$
$$+ 2\theta\alpha\left\{\alpha m_i + (1-\alpha)m_j\right\} = 0. \tag{4.9}$$

---

[1]Under flexible exchange rates, in contrast, monetary expansion would likely depreciate the nominal exchange rate by more than it raised prices domestically, depreciating the real exchange rate and causing jobs to be gained in the country expanding its money supply at the expense of the other. Thus, as discussed in Chapter 2, the sign of the transmission effect depends on the exchange rate regime; we will consider the case of flexible exchange rates in the next chapter.

Since the countries are identical, so must be their optimal policies; taking expectations and solving for the common optimal policy, we get

$$m^N = \frac{\gamma(1-\omega)}{\alpha\theta}k + \frac{\gamma(1-\omega)}{\gamma^2(1-\omega) + \alpha\theta}u. \tag{4.10}$$

So here in the absence of shocks there is a bias towards an overly expansionary monetary policy (the first term). If the central bank could precommit, it would respond only to shocks, and not systematically attempt to raise output above its equilibrium level. Doing so just creates higher inflation. But by assumption it cannot precommit.

Under **cooperation**, we assume that each country is given an equal weight in the objective function, so

$$L = \frac{1}{2}\left\{(y_1 - k)^2 + \theta\pi_1^2 + (y_2 - k)^2 + \theta\pi_2^2\right\}.$$

FOCs yield

$$m^C = \frac{\gamma}{\theta}k + \frac{\gamma}{\gamma^2 + \theta}u. \tag{4.11}$$

The cooperative solution does not depend on ω nor α, which capture the extent of output and inflation spillovers, because the objective function internalises the spillover effects. Comparing (4.10) and (4.11), we can note that if there are no spillovers (so both $\alpha = 1$ and $\omega = 0$), then the two solutions are the same. The intuition here is that these assumptions imply a situation of autarchy, where the two countries are essentially closed economies; cooperation is irrelevant, since what each country does has no effect on the other. It is also true that $m_i^C = m_i^N$ when $(1 - \omega) = \alpha$. Here, the spillovers do not change the closed-economy trade-off between the effects of money growth on inflation and output. This trade-off can be expressed in terms of a parameter $\delta \equiv (1 - \omega)/\alpha$. In the two cases cited above, $\delta = 1$.

Consider what happens if we decrease δ below one. Comparing the welfare of the Nash and Cooperative Equilibria, for either of the two countries, gives

$$L^N = \frac{\theta[\gamma^2 + \theta/\delta^2]}{[\gamma^2 + \theta/\delta]^2}u^2 + \frac{2\delta[\gamma^2 + \theta/\delta^2]}{\gamma^2 + \theta/\delta}ku + \frac{\theta + (\gamma\delta)^2}{\theta}k^2,$$

and

$$L^C = \frac{\theta}{\gamma^2 + \theta}u^2 + 2ku + \frac{\theta + \gamma^2}{\theta}k^2.$$

It is clear that the two expressions are equal when $\delta = 1$. However, the derivative of L^N with respect to δ, evaluated at $\delta = 1$, is positive when $u > 0$. Thus, decreasing δ below unity will (at least initially) unambiguously reduce the loss relative to the cooperative solution for a negative output shock. (It is also true that the expected loss will be greater for the cooperative solution, taking expectations over the mean-zero shock u, which introduces the variance of u into the first term and eliminates the second term). Thus, in this case, cooperation is actually harmful. For $\delta < 1$ the cooperative solution produces a greater inflation bias than the non-cooperative one (see the last terms in the expressions for L^C and L^N above). Under the noncooperative solution, there is a negative effect on the real exchange rate of expanding the money supply faster than in the neighbouring country, and this disincentive tends to keep down the rate of monetary expansion. Under the cooperative solution, however, the fact that both countries expand equally in a coordinated fashion removes this restraint.

Thus, cooperation can involve welfare costs as well as benefits (quite apart from any resource costs involved in negotiating and enforcing agreements): though it can enhance the flexibility to respond to symmetric unemployment shocks, it may also increase the inflation bias. Under certain circumstances, this can produce a deterioration of welfare relative to a Nash equilibrium, illustrating possible pitfalls of cooperation in a second-best world with an existing distortion (lack of precommitment and $k > 0$).

Chapter 5

Sustaining Coordination

5.1. Obstacles to Achieving Policy Coordination

The previous chapter considered gains from policy coordination in a framework where each country was only concerned about its own domestic variables, inflation and output, and where the effects of policies and shocks were known by all. If we relax these assumptions, then the rationale for policy coordination may be weakened. In order to consider these issues, we need to work with a more general model.

5.2. Conflict over Objectives

In addition to spillover effects that prevent a country operating independently to get to its second-best optimum when reacting to a supply shock, there may also be permanent inconsistencies in the targets of countries. For instance, countries may have a target for their real exchange rate. This may be explained by a desire to improve real income; if countries buy foreign goods or have debt denominated in foreign currency, then an appreciation of the real exchange rate means that the country is better off (absent any negative effects on output). However, a real appreciation of one country is the other's real depreciation, so that both cannot achieve their targets at the same time.

Let us now write the objective function as

$$L_i = y_i^2 + \theta\pi_i^2 + \phi z_i, \tag{5.1}$$

where z is the log of the real exchange rate (an increase indicates a depreciation) and $\phi > 0$. The rate of inflation will be given as before as a weighted average of domestic and foreign money growth:

$$\pi_i = \alpha m_i + (1 - \alpha)m_j, \tag{5.2}$$

where $j =$ the other country, while output is determined by money growth surprises plus the effect of the real exchange rate:

$$y_i = \gamma(m_i - m_i^e + \omega z_i) - u, \tag{5.3}$$

with $\omega > 0$.

Direct activity effects of foreign monetary expansion are ignored here, so, as discussed in Chapter 2, with flexible exchange rates foreign monetary expansion is negatively transmitted since it appreciates the home country's real exchange rate. We assume that the real exchange rate is determined by the difference of money growth rates:

$$z_i = m_i - m_j.$$

In this case, the Nash equilibrium can be obtained from the FOC

$$\frac{\partial L_i}{\partial m_i} = 2\gamma(1 + \omega) \left\{ \gamma[m_i - m_i^e + \omega(m_i - m_j)] - u \right\}$$
$$+ 2\theta\alpha[\alpha m_i + (1 - \alpha)m_j] + \phi = 0$$

yielding the solution

$$m^N = \frac{\gamma u}{\gamma^2 + \theta\alpha/(1+\omega)} - \frac{\phi}{2\theta\alpha}.$$

Thus, with a positive output shock ($u < 0$), the Nash equilibrium is even more contractionary than before because of the desire of each country to appreciate its exchange rate. Indeed, with a zero shock, there is a contractionary bias to monetary policy. However, with a negative output shock the real exchange rate objective may offset partially or completely the monetary expansion that is aimed at cushioning the shock.

The cooperative policy can be found by maximising the equally weighted average of the two countries' welfare functions. As noted above, with two countries, one country's appreciation is the other's depreciation: $z_i = -z_j$. Thus, the real exchange rate terms cancel out when the objective function is $(L_i + L_j)/2$, and the objective function under cooperation is identical to what it was in the previous chapter, with $k = 0$. The cooperative solution is easily calculated — cf. Equation (4.11):

$$m^C = \frac{\gamma u}{\gamma^2 + \theta}. \tag{5.4}$$

Here, then, the Nash is even farther from the cooperative solution when $u < 0$. But clearly for a positive value of u the expansionary bias of the Nash would tend to offset the contractionary effect of the conflict over real exchange rate objectives, and there is a point where the Nash and cooperative solutions would be equal.

5.3.   Model Uncertainty and/or Disagreement

It seems plausible that disagreement over how the economy works would reduce the scope for reaching agreement on policy coordination (Cooper, 1985). After all, if two countries cannot form a common view of the effects of their policies, then it is unlikely that they will see the advantages from a particular set of policy changes. Frankel and Rockett (1988) showed on the basis of the different multicountry models represented at a conference held at the Brookings Institution that disagreement about models made it likely that coordination (assuming that policy bargains on the basis of the different models could be reached) would reduce welfare, not increase it.

However, disagreement about the correct model and uncertainty are not the same thing. In the latter case, two countries may agree that the effects of policies are not precisely known, and still reach agreement over welfare-enhancing policies. In fact, uncertainty may provide an extra incentive to coordinate.

A simple example is sufficient to illustrate the latter point (see Ghosh and Masson, 1994, Chapter 3). Let us return to the case of the previous chapter, but assume further that countries target inflation only, which depends on domestic and foreign money growth, plus a common shock ε. So

$$L_i = \pi_i^2 \quad \text{and} \quad \pi_i = \alpha m_i + \beta m_j + \varepsilon,$$

and

$$L_j = \pi_j^2 \quad \text{and} \quad \pi_j = \alpha m_j + \beta m_i + \varepsilon.$$

Clearly, one instrument in each country is sufficient to hit the single target (zero) for inflation, provided that the shock is observed and the coefficients are known. Instead, let us assume that α and β are stochastic, with means $\bar{\alpha}$, $\bar{\beta} > 0$ and variances σ_α^2 and σ_β^2. It is further assumed that α and β are independent, both of each other and the shock ε, and that both countries have the same estimates of the means and variances. Furthermore, they observe the shock first, but have to choose their policies before knowing the realisation of α and β.

In this case, countries try to minimise the expected loss. The Nash equilibrium involves minimising it with respect to one's own instrument, taking the other one as given. Once again, the solution is simplified by noting that the two countries are identical in all respects, so their optimal policies are the same. The common money growth rate in the Nash equilibrium is given by

$$m^N = -\frac{1}{\overline{\alpha} + \overline{\beta} + \sigma_\alpha^2/\overline{\alpha}}\varepsilon. \tag{5.5}$$

Thus, when there is uncertainty about the effect of one's own policy instrument ($\sigma_\alpha^2 > 0$), monetary policy does not offset the inflationary shock fully [which would involve setting $m^N = -\varepsilon/(\overline{\alpha} + \overline{\beta})$ as in the certainty case] because the more active the use of monetary policy, the greater the risk of increasing the variance of inflation.

Under coordination, with equal weights in the joint objective function, optimal policy would minimise $L = L_1 + L_2$ jointly with respect to the two monetary policies. This yields a common rate of money growth

$$m^C = -\frac{1}{\overline{\alpha} + \overline{\beta} + (\sigma_\alpha^2 + \sigma_\beta^2)/(\overline{\alpha} + \overline{\beta})}\varepsilon. \tag{5.6}$$

The optimal coordinated policy (5.6) differs from the optimal unco-ordinated policy (5.5) as long as either σ_α^2 or σ_β^2 is non-zero, except for the special case where $\sigma_\alpha^2/\overline{\alpha} = \sigma_\beta^2/\overline{\beta}$. Under the assumptions made, the coordinated solution is Pareto optimal, and since it differs from the Nash solution, coordination therefore enhances welfare in the presence of parameter uncertainty. Some intuition can be pro-vided for this result by referring to a paper by Brainard (1967) on uncertainty and the effectiveness of policy which shows that if effects are uncertain, it is optimal to use more than one instrument to attain a single target. Coordination allows partial control over the foreign monetary instrument, and therefore has the potential to enhance welfare in this case.

In order to gauge the effect of increases in uncertainty, it is useful to distinguish between **transmission effects** of policies (β above) and their **domestic effects** (α above). An increase in uncertainty about the transmission effects (an increase in σ_β^2) unambiguously increases m^C for $\varepsilon > 0$ (making m^C less negative) while leaving m^N

unchanged. In contrast, the effect of an increase in uncertainty about domestic effects is ambiguous, since it increases both m^C and m^N. In the limit as $\sigma_\alpha^2 \to \infty$, the two policies become identical and reduce to complete policy inactivism: uncertainty about domestic effects would make it unwise to attempt to use monetary policy to offset inflation shocks to any extent whatsoever, and this is reflected in both coordinated and uncoordinated policies. In contrast, uncoordinated policies in the face of large transmission uncertainty $(\sigma_\beta^2 \to \infty)$ would continue to attempt to use monetary policy to hit the domestic inflation target, in the process inducing great variance in the other country's inflation rate and reducing welfare.

In the general case of many targets and instruments, with distortions such that coordination might lower welfare, it is impossible to obtain unambiguous analytical results. Whether coordination is welfare improving or not therefore becomes an empirical question. The empirical estimates in Ghosh and Masson (1994) suggest that taking account of the uncertainty facing policymakers increases substantially the expected gains from policy coordination. This may help to explain why coordination seems to occur in especially uncertain times associated with global economic crises. Masson (1992) presents a formal model that illustrates this point with respect to the October 1987 global stock market crash.

5.4. Institutions for Fostering Coordination

We have already touched on the issue of enforcement mechanisms to achieve the cooperative solution. It needs to be stressed that even if the optimal policy is agreed to, each country has an incentive to revert to its reaction function, which is the best response to the other country's policy. If both do so, we are back to the Nash equilibrium. While reputation and trigger strategies can enforce the cooperative equilibrium, another approach is to design institutions with enforcement features that may at least approach the welfare of the cooperative equilibrium.

5.4.1. *One-sided exchange rate pegs*

Canzoneri and Gray (1985) give the example of a unilateral peg of one currency to the other in a two-country world which, under some (quite restrictive) circumstances, can produce the same results as the cooperative equilibrium when there is a conflict over stabilisation. The idea is that there are institutions that would automatically yield good results; Canzoneri and Gray further design an incentive mechanism that would make maintaining the peg incentive compatible for the country doing so. The fixed exchange rate regime is modelled as a non-cooperative game in the context of a principal/agent problem, where the central bank is the agent for the government (or society) and is given a particular contract.

Let us assume that the home country is the one that is pegging to the foreign country. Society's objective function is given by (5.1), with $\phi = 0$. The central bank cares about society's loss L but is also given an additional incentive, in the form of a performance contract that mandates a transfer T under certain circumstances. The central bank thus minimises $L - T$, where the transfer T is defined over the change of the nominal exchange rate (s) and is given as follows:

$$T(s) = \alpha \quad \text{if } s = 0,$$
$$T(s) = \alpha - c \quad \text{otherwise.}$$

Thus, this resembles the penalties on the authorities in second-generation currency crisis models, discussed in Chapter 2. c is a positive number and is chosen to be large enough that T exceeds L for all realisations of policies and shocks.

It is important to be clear on the timing of the game:

(i) society commits to a contract for the home country,
(ii) expectations of money growth are formed,

(iii) the supply shock is realised,
(iv) foreign policymaker chooses m^*,
 (v) the home central bank chooses m,
(vi) macroeconomic outcomes are realised.

It is assumed that the nominal exchange rate change is proportional to the difference in money growth rates, with $\rho > 0$:

$$s = \rho(m - m^*).$$

The performance contract will force the home central bank to choose the same money growth as the foreign central bank, to keep the exchange rate fixed, since s is zero if and only if $m = m^*$. Faced with this reaction function from the home country, the foreign country realises that $z \equiv s + \pi - \pi^* = 0$ whatever policy is set, so any effects on z in the optimisation decision can be ignored. Thus, the first order condition is

$$\frac{\partial L^*}{\partial m^*} = 2\gamma[\gamma(m^* - m^{*e}) - u] + 2\theta m^* = 0,$$

but this yields a solution that is identical to the cooperative equilibrium, for both the home and the foreign country. Letting the F superscript denote the fixed exchange rate regime, then

$$m^F = \frac{\gamma u}{\gamma^2 + \theta}.$$

Thus, the incentive contract on the pegging central bank ensures that for a symmetric supply shock, the cooperative solution is replicated [see Equation (5.4)].

While this is a clever set-up, it is important to realise its limitations. It only holds for a symmetric supply shock, absent any conflict over objectives. Clearly, there are also asymmetric shocks. Instead of replicating the cooperative solution for all shocks, the best one can aim for is a regime that on average, given the expected correlation of shocks, does better than another. This leads into our discussion of exchange rate regimes and monetary unions in Part III of this book.

Part III
Common Currency Areas

Chapter 6

Monetary Integration

6.1. Choice of Currency Regime

There are two related literatures, one on whether to join a currency area and the other, assuming a country retains its own currency, on the optimal degree of flexibility to allow for its exchange rate. The degree of flexibility is assumed to be chosen by the monetary authorities. The two issues are of course related, since a common currency is the limiting case of lack of flexibility. However, a common currency is not exactly the same as a fixed exchange rate, because sharing a currency may involve lower transactions costs for trade between the affected countries. In addition, a fixed rate may not be completely credible, since the monetary authorities may change the parity (despite denying any intention of doing so).

6.1.1. *Fixed versus flexible exchange rates*

The literature on optimal flexibility considers whether shocks to an economy are real or monetary, and the degree of indexation of the economy. If the economy is predominantly hit by domestic nominal shocks, then an external target (like the exchange rate) is better than a domestic target like the money supply. The optimal degree of flexibility of the exchange rate depends on the ratio of the variances of shocks, and in general it would be optimal for the exchange rate to be neither perfectly fixed nor perfectly flexible. However, once one introduces time consistency problems, fixity of the exchange rate may then allow importing credibility from a foreign central bank and may be welfare superior. This argument was much used in the early days of the EMS when countries like France and Italy benefitted from a link of their currencies to the deutsche mark in their attempts to lower inflation, but the 1992–1993 crises showed its limitations. Furthermore, sharing a common currency may have advantages such as reduced transactions costs that go beyond those from a fixed rate.

6.1.2. *Optimum currency areas*

The optimum currency area (OCA) literature, started by Mundell (1961), asks the following questions: What explains the number of currencies, and what is it that makes currency areas work smoothly? Is the world an OCA? Mundell's analysis focusses on labour mobility as a key factor in making currency areas work: when two regions sharing the same currency face different shocks, if unemployed workers in the unfavourably affected region can move to jobs in the better-off region, income (and welfare) losses can be minimised. Thus, with labour mobility membership in a common currency area does not entail large costs.

Other factors that would make currency areas work include fiscal transfers between regions, similarity of production structures, and a high degree of integration between regions. However, fiscal transfers can produce "welfare dependency" of worse off regions (e.g., Canada's Maritime Provinces). Even if fiscal transfers are intended to compensate for shocks (and hence should even out in the long run), this is difficult to achieve in practice. And permanent transfers may inhibit adjustment rather than providing insurance against asymmetric shocks.

The likelihood of asymmetric shocks is decreased if regions are diversified, rather than depending on production of a single good; shocks to diversified regions will tend to average out, and resemble those of other diversified regions.

The degree of openness has sometimes been used as an argument in favour of fixed rates: the argument is that more open economies will benefit little from the use of the exchange rate to cushion real shocks but will suffer much from the inflationary consequences. This argument does not stand up to more general examination. But it is true that the more open the economy, the more the use of an international currency will save on transactions costs.

Indeed, one needs to look at the benefits of a common currency as well as the costs. The benefits will depend on the choice of the currency peg: adopting a stable, convertible, and internationally used currency (as an anchor or reserve currency) issued by a large country will be more beneficial than adopting the currency of a small, poor, or unstable country. Benefits of a common currency include lowering of transactions costs and providing a stable reference for calculating relative prices, especially if the domestic central bank does not benefit from credibility, while the foreign central bank does (e.g., the Bundesbank).

But the purely economic factors certainly do not explain the fact that there are so many currencies, as Mundell implicitly recognised: for political reasons, countries in most cases keep their own currencies, the exceptions being the euro zone, the CFA franc zone in Africa (which survives for historical reasons), the Eastern Caribbean Currency Union, and a few cases of dollarisation. Mundell's answer was that probably the western region of both the United States and Canada and the eastern region of the two countries were each an OCA, but for political reasons it was impossible to have currencies that overlapped national boundaries; thus the issue was how to make the existing currency areas based on the US and Canadian dollars work. The European experience however has changed the view that maintaining one's own currency is essential, and if this new attitude prevails in other parts of the world in the future, it may lead to more monetary unions and thus lower the number of currencies.

6.1.3. *Formal models of currency unions*

Creating general OCA models is difficult, because of the number of factors (mentioned above), and because to be relevant, monetary models need to include frictions and savings of transactions costs when countries use the same currency. Both factors are very hard to model. But there is a new interest in formal models to address the issues thrown up by Europe, namely the interaction of monetary and fiscal policies.

In some of the literature, transactions costs are modelled as "iceberg costs" — the real resources lost in transportation (by analogy with melting along the way) — but clearly only some of this involves currency exchange. Empirical estimates of the cost due to currency exchange in Europe were small (and based on estimates of foreign exchange market spreads and profits of dealers) — at most half a percent of GDP or so. Costs per transaction might well be larger in less financially developed economies, but on the other hand Europe has more internal trade than other regions, so the overall saving from a single country in Europe is likely to be higher.

6.1.4. *Types of monetary integration*

It is important to distinguish various ways a link to a foreign currency can be used as the domestic monetary policy regime.

(i) A **currency peg**, in which the monetary authorities undertake to restrict the fluctuation of the country's currency against some reference currency (or basket of currencies).

(ii) A **currency board**, which is an intermediate case between a currency peg and adoption of the foreign currency, because the central bank (CB) gives up all autonomy but the country retains its own currency, rigidly linked to the foreign one. This means that the home country still can generate *seigniorage*, that is, extract real resources for the government when the money supply expands.

(iii) **Dollarisation** (or by extension, euroisation, though dollarisation is often used to refer to the general case) means that a country unilaterally adopts a foreign currency. Alesina and Barro (2002) consider this case.

(iv) A **monetary union**, which involves sharing a common currency, while jointly deciding on monetary policy. Thus, a monetary union is in principle symmetric. How decisions are made and seigniorage divided need to be specified.

6.1.5. *Why modelling fiscal/monetary interaction is important*

A CB under the control of the fiscal authorities may be forced to provide monetary financing of fiscal deficits, especially if other sources of government financing dry up. This has often been true in the past in developing countries, though development of financial markets makes it less prevalent now. It is sometimes argued that statutory independence of the CB is sufficient to insulate the latter from pressures to monetise fiscal deficits. Experience has shown this not to be true, and the view taken by the founders of the euro zone was that extra safeguards are required in the form of limitations on the power of fiscal authorities to run large deficits. Within the Economic and Monetary Union (EMU), such limits are embodied in the Maastricht Excessive Deficits Procedures and the Stability and Growth Pact (see Box 6.1).

Box 6.1. Limits on Fiscal Deficits within the European Union

The 1991 Maastricht Treaty on EMU, in addition to prohibiting the European Central Bank from providing monetary financing to governments, also includes provisions for limiting fiscal deficits. In particular, Article 104 of the amended Treaty establishing the European Community specifies that

1. Member States shall avoid excessive government deficits.
2. The Commission shall monitor the development of the budgetary situation and of the stock of government debt in the Member States with a view to identifying gross errors. In particular it shall examine compliance with budgetary discipline on the basis of the following two criteria:
   (a) whether the ratio of the planned or actual government deficit to gross domestic product exceeds a reference value, unless — either the ratio has declined substantially and continuously and reached a level that comes close to the reference value; — or, alternatively, the excess over the reference value is only exceptional and temporary and the ratio remains close to the reference value;
   (b) whether the ratio of government debt to gross domestic product exceeds a reference value, unless the ratio is sufficiently diminishing and approaching the reference value at a satisfactory pace.

The reference values for government deficits and public debt are respectively 3 percent of GDP and 60 percent of GDP.

Though the Treaty provides for consultation and sanctions against countries that exceed those reference values, the Stability and Growth Pact, agreed in 1997, further strengthened the procedures and provided for the possibility of sanctions of up to 0.5 percent of GDP for countries in the euro zone having excessive deficits.

In practice, many of the EU countries have had trouble meeting the ceilings for deficits and debt, including the largest euro zone economies, Germany and France. Consequently, the euro zone countries collectively

(Continued)

Box 6.1. (*Continued*)

have been unwilling to apply the sanctions which the SGP prescribes. After debate concerning the best way to reform of the SGP, a compromise reached in 2005 gave countries more latitude to exceed temporarily the reference levels. Concern about the need to impose fiscal discipline on euro zone countries persists, however.

Source: European Commission website.

There are several reasons why statutory CB independence may not be enough. First, politicians have been known to subvert that statutory independence; de facto independence may not be absolute when governments name central bankers and can use various means to influence them. Second, even if the CB has independent use of its instruments to achieve agreed objectives, if those objectives include variables which are also influenced by fiscal policy, then the CB may be led to an excessively expansionary policy, especially if fiscal policy has a strategic advantage. This is discussed further in the next chapter. For instance, one of the concerns of the drafters of the Maastricht Treaty creating the euro zone was that politicians might ignore fiscal discipline if they expected that the ECB would not want to face the output losses from a major default on government debt ("too big to fail"). Thus, they tried to reduce the likelihood of such a situation emerging.

Problems of spillovers of fiscal deficits onto monetary policy may be especially severe in a monetary union because the costs of higher inflation are paid not just by the country concerned but also by others in the union. Thus, a monetary union increases the scope for "free rider" problems.

6.1.6. *Recent models of fiscal/monetary policy interaction in a common currency area*

Relevant models in this area consider the interaction of a single regional monetary policy and national fiscal policies in a monetary union (comparing the monetary union to the situation with independent monetary, as well as fiscal, policies). There are many modelling choices that need to be made:

(i) **Fiscal dominance versus monetary independence.** In the first case, the CB does not set its own targets or control its instruments but acts under the control of fiscal authorities and in particular is subordinated to the need to finance fiscal deficits. My own paper with Xavier Debrun and Catherine Pattillo, discussed below, falls into this category. Other related literature concerns the fiscal theory of the price level, in which prices move to satisfy the government intertemporal budget constraint [see Woodford (1995)].

(ii) **Precommitment.** Even though the CB may be independent, we can distinguish between the one able to precommit (in the sense of the time consistency literature) and the one that cannot, and is forced instead to operate discretionary policy. Because of a Barro–Gordon distortion, the optimal policy will generally not be the discretionary policy. Monetary union may be a solution to this problem, if the monetary union's CB is able to precommit. Other proposed solutions are "Walsh" contracts (where society is the principal, the CB the agent) or appointment of conservative central bankers.

(iii) **The rules of the game.** Formal models also need to define the rules of the game of monetary–fiscal interaction:

- Who plays first?
- Are national fiscal policies coordinated among themselves?
- Are national fiscal policies constrained by a rule of some sort, like the Stability and Growth Pact (and how enforced)?
- How are decisions at the CB taken?
- How is seigniorage distributed?

6.2. Monetary Union with a Dependent CB

We will start by considering the case of a dependent CB, modelled in Debrun *et al.* (2005). The case of a dependent CB is relevant for most African central banks and proposals for African monetary unions [they are reviewed in Masson and Pattillo (2004)]. In practice, monetary growth has often been driven by the needs to finance governments. There is no reason to think that a regional central bank would be any different, but the multilateral context would dilute to some extent the influence of any individual government. As we will see below, this helps provide a partial offset to the inflationary bias.

The model extends the Barro–Gordon model to capture the interaction of monetary and fiscal policies in the simplest possible way while including essential features. In order to include an effect of taxes on output, it uses a variant of the supply equation due to Alesina and Tabellini (1987). The supply equation is modified to incorporate cross-border effects of inflation surprises; these effects of course are internalised within a monetary union or a dollarised economy. The model also incorporates a budget constraint that requires government spending to be financed by taxes or seigniorage, and a government objective function that depends on inflation, the tax rate, government spending, and output. The budget constraint includes not only explicit government spending but also a wedge (which differs across countries) due to wasteful spending, corruption, and inefficient tax collection; in addition, countries are assumed to differ in their fiscal objectives. The objective function targets an inflation rate that depends inversely on the supply shock, introducing a role for stabilisation policy. The model is described in more detail in Debrun and Masson (2005) and Debrun *et al.* (2005).

6.2.1. *The supply equation*

Output in country i (in logs) depends on its own inflation surprises, minus the tax rate, and on inflation surprises in other countries, where $\theta_{i,k}$ captures the strength of transmission effects, which are assumed to be negative so that a monetary expansion abroad lowers domestic output:

$$y_i = c(\pi_i - \pi_i^e - \tau_i) - \sum_{k=1}^{n} \theta_{i,k} c(\pi_k - \pi_k^e) + \epsilon_i, \ i = 1, \ldots, n. \quad (6.1)$$

For convenience, the level of output in the absence of taxes, shocks, or inflation surprises is set equal to zero. It is assumed that $\theta_{i,k} \geq 0, \sum_{k=1}^{n} \theta_{i,k} \leq 1$, and $\theta_{i,i} \equiv 0$.

6.2.2. *The government's budget constraint*

Government spending (divided by GDP), g_i, is financed by taxes τ_i or by seigniorage, the latter being equal to the rate of inflation times the inflation tax base, μ. μ is notionally the money/income ratio, and is taken to be a parameter. The parameter ϕ_i measures the proportion of seigniorage accruing to the country. It is equal to zero in the case of dollarisation, and unity when a country has its own currency or is a member of a monetary union (thus, seigniorage in a monetary union is assumed to be divided up on the basis of relative GDP levels). An amount δ_i of taxes (as a share of GDP) is siphoned off and does not go to useful government spending, due to waste, corruption, or inefficient tax collection.

$$g_i = \mu \phi_i \pi_i + \tau_i - \delta_i. \quad (6.2)$$

Actual government spending g_i may not be equal to government spending objectives $\tilde{g}_i$ because of the costs of raising finance and wasteful spending. We can combine spending objectives with the corruption/inefficiency distortion, giving a single measure of fiscal (in)discipline:

$$F_i \equiv \tilde{g}_i + \delta_i. \quad (6.3)$$

We call this the **financing need**. It is assumed that $0 \leq F_i \leq 1$: the financing need is positive, but cannot exceed GDP.

6.2.3. *The government's objective function*

The objective function is assumed to be quadratic in deviations of inflation, taxes, and government spending from their targets, and linear in the logarithm of output. The target for inflation is inversely proportional to the supply shock, $\tilde{\pi}_i = -\eta\varepsilon_i$; the bliss point for taxes is zero, while that for government spending is a constant, $\tilde{g}_i$:

$$U_i = -\frac{1}{2}\{a(\pi_i + \eta\varepsilon_i)^2 + b\tau_i^2 + \gamma(g_i - \tilde{g}_i)^2\} + y_i. \qquad (6.4)$$

6.2.4. *Optimal fiscal policy*

The private sector is assumed to form its expectations before the realisation of the supply shock but with perfect knowledge of the government's objective function. The CB, whether a national or supranational one, maximises (6.4) with respect to inflation after observing the supply shock; we will derive optimal monetary policies. Fiscal policy takes the rate of inflation as given and maximises (6.4) with respect to τ_i subject to (6.2), which yields values for g_i. Optimal fiscal policies, conditional on the rate of inflation, are given by

$$\tau_i^* = \frac{\gamma}{b+\gamma}F_i - \frac{\gamma}{b+\gamma}\mu\phi_i\pi_i - \frac{c}{b+\gamma}, \qquad (6.5)$$

$$g_i^* = \tilde{g}_i - \frac{b}{b+\gamma}F_i + \frac{b}{b+\gamma}\mu\phi_i\pi_i - \frac{c}{b+\gamma}. \qquad (6.6)$$

Thus, the sum of explicit government spending objectives and tax diversion (the financing need F_i) increases taxes, but less than proportionately, and also drives a wedge between actual spending and the spending objective. Higher inflation, to the extent that the government earns seigniorage ($\phi_i > 0$), leads to lower taxes and higher government spending. Both are lowered by a constant amount that incorporates the depressive effect of taxes on output (the last term).

6.2.5.   *Optimal monetary policies*

The rate of inflation chosen depends on the monetary policy regime. In the case of autonomy (**independent currency**), the relevant objective is simply (6.4), $\phi_i = 1$ (the country retains seigniorage), and the first-order condition yields the following optimal (second best) policy:

$$\pi_i^I = \frac{\gamma\mu b}{\Lambda}F_i + \frac{b+\gamma+\gamma\mu}{\Lambda}c - \frac{a(b+\gamma)\eta}{\Lambda}\varepsilon_i, \qquad (6.7)$$

where $\Lambda \equiv a(b+\gamma)+\gamma\mu^2 b$. Thus, higher financing needs raise inflation (since the CB has the same fiscal objectives as does the government), while monetary policy tends to lean against supply shocks (the last term). Inflation is suboptimally high because of the CB's inability to precommit not to produce surprise inflation (the second term).

   If there is a **monetary union** (whose members belong to the set h, while those outside belong to set H), then the supranational central bank is assumed to maximise a weighted average of member countries' objective functions, with weights ω_j^h (which sum to one over j) based on relative GDP within h:

$$U_h = -\frac{1}{2}\sum_{j\epsilon h}\omega_j^h\{a(\pi_h + \eta\varepsilon_j)^2 + b\tau_j^2 + \gamma(g_j - \widetilde{g}_j)^2\} + \sum_{j\epsilon h}\omega_j^h y_j.$$

$$(6.8)$$

   In addition, each country's supply function is modified by the membership in the monetary union, because the latter internalises some of the inflation spillovers.

$$y_j = c\left(1 - \sum_{k\epsilon h}\theta_{j,k}\right)(\pi_h - \pi_h^e) - c\tau_j - c\sum_{k\epsilon H}\theta_{j,k}(\pi_k - \pi_k^e) + \epsilon_j,$$

$$j \in h, \quad (6.9)$$

where, as specified earlier, H is the closure of the set h. Since countries get their GDP shares of seigniorage, $\phi_j = 1$, $\forall j \in h$. The rate of inflation that optimizes (6.8) for the monetary union h, common across all the countries in the union, depends on weighted averages of the member countries' fiscal targets and the supply shocks, as well as the inflation spillovers internalised in the union. It is convenient to write these aggregates as follows:

$$F_A^h \equiv \sum_{j \in h} \omega_j^h F_j, \tag{6.10}$$

$$\varepsilon_A^h \equiv \sum_{j \in h} \omega_j^h \varepsilon_j, \tag{6.11}$$

$$\theta_A^h \equiv \sum_{j \in h} \omega_j^h \sum_{k \in h} \theta_{j,k}. \tag{6.12}$$

Then, the optimal rate of inflation in monetary union h is given by

$$\pi_h^* = \frac{\gamma \mu b}{\Lambda} F_A^h + \frac{\left(1 - \theta_A^h\right)(b + \gamma) + \gamma \mu}{\Lambda} c - \frac{a(b + \gamma)\eta}{\Lambda} \varepsilon_A^h. \tag{6.13}$$

Comparison with (6.7) shows that a monetary union's inflation rate depends on average fiscal and shock variables rather than solely that of the country alone, and also that the incentive to raise inflation (the middle term) is reduced by a proportion of the amount that inflation spillovers are internalised in the union.

In the case of **dollarisation**, country i simply adopts another country's currency, or the currency of a monetary union, without affecting their monetary policy. Thus, country i takes as given to it some external rate of inflation, and $\phi_i = 0$ since it does not obtain any seigniorage. This affects optimal fiscal policies, given by (6.5) and (6.6) which now become independent of the rate of inflation.

6.3. Choice of Monetary Regime

We assume that the choice among the three regimes — monetary independence, monetary union, or dollarisation — depends on which one produces the highest expected welfare (presumably averaged over the business cycle, or longer period), subject to the caveat that monetary union also requires the approval of existing members to join (analysed below). We proceed to derive expressions for these expected values.

Whatever the rate of inflation, the expressions for the optimal values for taxes and spending can be substituted into the government's objective function, and expected utility can be seen to depend on the first two moments of the rate of inflation and the correlation of inflation with the country's supply shock:

$$EU_i(\pi) = -\frac{1}{2} \left\{ \begin{array}{l} \left[a + \dfrac{b\gamma}{b+\gamma}\phi_i^2\mu^2 \right] E(\pi^2) + 2a\eta E(\pi\varepsilon_i) \\[2ex] + a\eta^2 E(\varepsilon_i^2) + \dfrac{b\gamma}{b+\gamma}F_i^2 \\[2ex] - \dfrac{c^2}{b+\gamma} + \dfrac{2c\gamma}{b+\gamma}F_i - \dfrac{2\gamma\phi_i\mu}{b+\gamma}[bF_i+c]E(\pi) \end{array} \right\}.$$

$$(6.14)$$

The three regimes differ with respect to the mean and variance of inflation and its correlation with i's supply shock. It is useful to introduce notation: let $\overline{h}$ be a monetary union that country i is considering joining, and if it does join, let h be the monetary union, including i (thus, h is the set $\overline{h}$ plus country i). So before i joins, monetary policy $\pi_{\overline{h}}^*$ is set to reflect average conditions of the existing members, in particular $F_A^{\overline{h}}$, $\varepsilon_A^{\overline{h}}$, and $\theta_A^{\overline{h}}$, and this is the rate of inflation that i will adopt if it dollarises because it will have no influence over the monetary policy of the existing union. If instead i becomes part of the monetary union, then its inflation rate will be π_h^*, which will depend on the averages F_A^h, ε_A^h, and θ_A^h that include i.

Under autonomy, the optimal inflation rate is given by (6.7), while for dollarisation or a monetary union that includes i, the optimal inflation rate is given by (6.13), with subscripts either $\overline{h}$ or h, respectively. From these, we can easily derive the required moments of inflation and its correlation with i's supply shock (expressions for these moments under the three regimes are given in the Appendix to this chapter). These expressions can then be substituted into (6.14) to get the expected utility from the regimes, taking into account differences in access to seigniorage between dollarisation ($\phi_i = 0$) on the one hand and monetary union or an independent currency ($\phi_i = 1$) on the other. Some intuition can be gained by from simplified expressions that substitute for the variance and/or covariance of inflation but not its mean. The gain from **dollarisation** relative to an independent currency can be written

$$DN_i = -\frac{1}{2}\left\{ a\left[E\left(\left(\pi_{\overline{h}}^*\right)^2\right) - E\left(\left(\pi_i^I\right)^2\right)\right]\right.$$
$$+ 2a\eta\left[E\left(\pi_{\overline{h}}^*\varepsilon_i\right) - E\left(\pi_i^I\varepsilon_i\right)\right] - \frac{b\gamma\mu^2 a^2(b+\gamma)\eta^2}{\Lambda^2}\mathrm{var}(\varepsilon_i)$$
$$\left. + \frac{\gamma\mu}{b+\gamma}E\left(\pi_i^I\right)\left[2(bF_i + c) - b\mu E\left(\pi_i^I\right)\right]\right\}. \qquad (6.15)$$

Note that, if inflation is the same in the two regimes, then the net gain will depend only on the last two terms within { }. (Note that the whole expression is preceded by a minus sign.) The first of these terms captures a gain from dollarisation, *ceteris paribus*, because the variance of inflation when the country runs its own currency depends on the variance of supply shocks, and inflation variance increases the variance of government spending. Since dollarisation eliminates seigniorage, it eliminates this source of disutility. The last term within {} will typically be positive, i.e., reducing the utility from dollarisation because of the expected loss of seigniorage. Indeed, $bF_i + c > b\mu E(\pi_i^I)$ implies that inflation is not high enough to provide revenue to accommodate all spending needs when taxes are zero [this can be seen from Equation. (6.6)]. Thus, loss of seigniorage has welfare costs. This is assumed to be the relevant case, and if it is true, then *a fortiori* the last term in (6.15) will be positive.

The gain from **monetary union** relative to an independent currency can be written:

$$MU_i = -\frac{1}{2}\left\{\left[E\left(\pi_h^*\right) - E\left(\pi_i^I\right)\right]\frac{\Lambda}{b+\gamma}\left[E\left(\pi_h^*\right) - E\left(\pi_i^I\right) + \frac{2(b+\gamma)c}{\Lambda}\right]\right.$$
$$\left. + \frac{a^2\eta^2(b+\gamma)}{\Lambda}\left[\mathrm{var}\left(\varepsilon_A^h\right) - 2\mathrm{cov}\left(\varepsilon_i, \varepsilon_A^h\right) + \mathrm{var}(\varepsilon_i)\right]\right\} \qquad (6.16)$$

The last term is positive, equal to zero only if the shocks are of equal variance and perfectly correlated.

If the last term is zero, then the remaining term is proportional to the difference in expected inflation rates in a monetary union relative to having an independent currency. Monetary union will be more attractive than an independent currency provided

$$-\frac{2(b+\gamma)c}{\Lambda} < E\left(\pi_h^*\right) - E\left(\pi_i^I\right) < 0. \qquad (6.17)$$

In the absence of asymmetric shocks, a country will want to join a monetary union if doing so leads to somewhat lower inflation, but inflation cannot be too low, otherwise the loss of seigniorage revenue offsets the gain from reducing the distortion due to the lack of monetary policy precommitment. When there are no asymmetric shocks and inflation rates are the same, then country i is just indifferent between joining and retaining its currency; this differs from dollarisation, where even at the same inflation rate, there will in general be a welfare gain or loss.

Of course, if shocks are not perfectly correlated, then any gain from lower inflation may be partially or totally offset by the suboptimal response to shocks from the perspective of country i of the monetary union's inflation rate. In the general case, monetary union will be preferred to an independent currency iff

$$-\frac{(b+\gamma)c}{\Lambda} - \Psi < E\left(\pi_h^*\right) - E\left(\pi_i^I\right) < -\frac{(b+\gamma)c}{\Lambda} + \Psi, \qquad (6.18)$$

where $\Psi \equiv [(b+\gamma)/\Lambda]\sqrt{c^2 - a^2\eta^2[\text{var}(\varepsilon_A^h) - 2\text{cov}(\varepsilon_i, \varepsilon_A^h) + \text{var}(\varepsilon_i)]}$. If the asymmetry of shocks is too great, then Ψ may not be a real number, which would imply that there would be no range of values for inflation for which monetary union would be preferred to an independent currency.

It is convenient to write the results of the full substitution of expressions for the moments in terms of two variables, x and y, that capture the extent that trade intensity and financing needs would increase as a result of i's potential membership in the monetary union. In particular, noting that $\theta_{i,h}$ is the amount country i trades with monetary union h, and F_i is country i's financing need, let

$$x \equiv \theta_{i,h} - \theta_A^{\bar{h}},$$
$$y \equiv F_i - F_A^{\bar{h}}.$$

In terms of these variables, the difference in inflation rates can be written:

$$E\left(\pi_h^*\right) - E\left(\pi_i^I\right) = -\frac{\gamma\mu b}{\Lambda}(1 - \omega_i^h)y - \frac{(b+\gamma)c}{\Lambda}\left(\theta_A^{\bar{h}} + \omega_i^h x\right).$$

The condition for monetary union to increase utility [expression (6.18)] then becomes

$$\frac{(b+\gamma)c - \Lambda\Psi}{\gamma\mu b} < \left(1 - \omega_i^h\right)y + \frac{(b+\gamma)c}{\gamma\mu b}\left(\theta_A^{\bar{h}} + \omega_i^h x\right) < \frac{(b+\gamma)c + \Lambda\Psi}{\gamma\mu b}.$$

$$(6.19)$$

6.4. Utility of Existing Members of a Monetary Union

However, country i's joining monetary union $\bar{h}$ to form the larger union h may not be compatible with the interests of the existing members. We can examine the expected utility of country j in monetary union $\bar{h}$ from the admission of country i using the earlier framework. We will assume that country j is the median country, that countries are all the same size, and that the distribution of financing needs is symmetric so that $F_j = F_A^{\bar{h}}$. We can then calculate how j's utility will change as a result of inflation being given by π_h^* rather than $\pi_{\bar{h}}^*$. Substitution for the moments of inflation in the two cases yields the following expression for the change in j's utility from the admission of country i:

$$A \equiv EU_j\left(\pi_h^*\right) - EU_j\left(\pi_{\bar{h}}^*\right) = -\frac{1}{2}\left\{\left[E\left(\pi_h^*\right) - E\left(\pi_{\bar{h}}^*\right)\right]\right.$$
$$\times \left[\frac{\gamma\mu b\omega_i^h y}{b+\gamma} + 2\left(1 - \theta_A^{\bar{h}}\right)c - \omega_i^h c x\right]$$

$$+ \frac{a^2\eta^2}{\Lambda}(b+\gamma)\left[\operatorname{var}\left(\varepsilon_A^h\right) - \operatorname{var}\left(\varepsilon_A^{\overline{h}}\right)\right.$$

$$\left. - 2\operatorname{cov}\left(\varepsilon_j, \varepsilon_A^h\right) + 2\operatorname{cov}\left(\varepsilon_j, \varepsilon_A^{\overline{h}}\right)\right]\bigg\}. \tag{6.20}$$

Suppose that variances and covariances are unaffected by the admission of i to the monetary union, so that the last term is zero; then j's decision will rest on the sign of the first term, which needs to be negative. Since

$$E(\pi_h^*) - E(\pi_{\overline{h}}^*) = \frac{\gamma\mu b}{\Lambda}w_i^h y - \frac{c(b+\gamma)}{\Lambda}w_i^h x,$$

inflation will decline iff $y < (b+\gamma)cx/\gamma\mu b$. Combining this with the second factor in (6.20), we see that $A > 0$ requires that

$$-\frac{2\left(1 - \theta_A^{\overline{h}}\right)(b+\gamma)c}{\gamma\mu b w_i^h} < y - \frac{(b+\gamma)cx}{\gamma\mu b} < 0. \tag{6.21}$$

If country i is equal in fiscal discipline and trade intensity to the median existing member (i.e., $x = y = 0$), then country j would be just indifferent between admitting i or excluding it if variances and covariances are unaffected. To the extent that country i is small ($w_i^h \to 0$), the leftmost inequality of (6.21) ceases to bind.

In general, admission of i will affect the variance of the monetary union's shock and j's covariance with it. The range of x and y values for which the median country in a monetary union would be willing to admit a new member in the general case is

$$-\left(1 - \theta_A^{\overline{h}}\right)c - \Sigma < w_i^h\left[\frac{\gamma\mu b}{b+\gamma}y - cx\right] < -\left(1 - \theta_A^{\overline{h}}\right)c + \Sigma, \tag{6.22}$$

where

$$\Sigma \equiv \sqrt{\begin{aligned}&\left(1 - \theta_A^{\overline{h}}\right)^2 c^2 - w_i^h a^2 \eta^2 \left[w_i^h\left(\operatorname{var}(\varepsilon_i) + \operatorname{var}\left(\varepsilon_A^{\overline{h}}\right)\right)\right.\\ &\left. - 2\operatorname{cov}\left(\varepsilon_i, \varepsilon_A^{\overline{h}}\right)\right) + 2\left(\operatorname{cov}\left(\varepsilon_i, \varepsilon_A^{\overline{h}}\right) + \operatorname{cov}\left(\varepsilon_j, \varepsilon_A^{\overline{h}}\right)\right.\\ &\left. - \operatorname{cov}(\varepsilon_i, \varepsilon_j) - \operatorname{var}\left(\varepsilon_A^{\overline{h}}\right)\right)\Big].\end{aligned}}$$

If Σ does not yield a real solution because effects of admitting i on variances and covariances are too unfavourable, then there is no range of values for x and y for which country j will be willing to admit country i. The size of country i however also makes a difference: as it goes to zero, Σ by necessity yields a real value, and the left inequality of (6.22) becomes non-binding (since the LHS is negative). As for the extent of fiscal discipline, it can be less than the average in the monetary union ($y < 0$), but only if i increases the trade intensity of the monetary union ($x > 0$). At $(x, y) = (0, 0)$, A is increasing in x and decreasing in y: more trade with $\bar{h}$ makes i a more attractive candidate for membership, less fiscal discipline makes it a less attractive one.

The complete expression for A after substitution of the variances and covariances is given in the Appendix.

6.5. Feasible Monetary Regimes

The above analysis of potential welfare gains for i of abandoning its independent currency in favour of dollarisation or membership in a monetary union, and the incentives for countries in the monetary union to admit i, allow us to characterise in (x, y) space the monetary regimes that are likely to emerge, with reference to a particular potential partner (single country or existing monetary union). If a country is very different from the potential partner in terms of fiscal discipline (very disciplined or indisciplined), then it will not want to join with it in monetary union (or dollarise). The more i trades with the potential union, the more attractive it will be for i to join that union. Conversely, greater discipline and higher trade will make i a more attractive candidate for the median country j in monetary union $\bar{h}$. There will be a range of values where country i would like to join a monetary union, but will not be admitted. In this case, its choice will be between dollarisation and an independent currency. Dollarisation will be attractive if i faces a high variance of supply shocks and does not require a large amount of seigniorage.

The formation of a monetary union must be both **desirable** from the point of view of the country joining (6.19) and **acceptable** to the median country within the union (6.22). We call monetary unions that satisfy both conditions **feasible** monetary unions. In contrast, dollarisation only requires that welfare of the country dollarising increase.

Figures 6.1 and 6.2 give illustrations in (x, y) space of a region where monetary unions are feasible. In Figure 6.1, the upper and lower slightly downward sloping lines are the upper and lower boundaries of the **desirable** region where country i would want to join a monetary union with median country j, while the region to the right of the upward sloping line that intersects the axes close to the origin defines the values for x and y which make i **acceptable** to country j. Therefore the area to the right of it and between the two

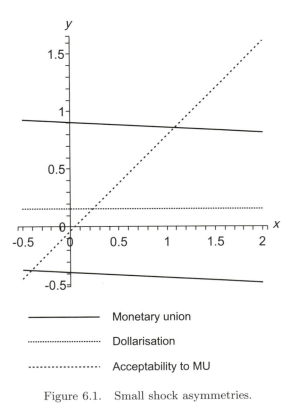

Figure 6.1.   Small shock asymmetries.

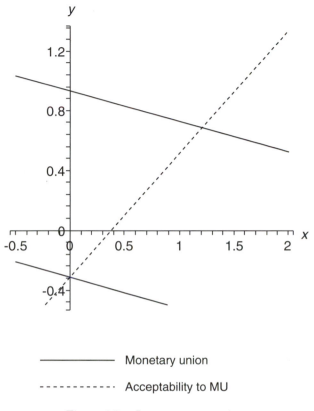

Monetary union
------------- Acceptability to MU

Figure 6.2.   Larger asymmetries.

downward sloping lines defines the **feasible region**. The area below
the horizontal line that intersects the y axis at about 0.15 is the
region where i would want to dollarise and adopt the currency of the
monetary union $\bar{h}$. It is below the upper limit of the monetary union
region, because dollarisation implies loss of seigniorage; at high values for y (and hence for the financing need F) the loss of seigniorage
would be too costly.

Figure 6.2 assumes that country i is larger and has more
asymmetric shocks with respect to the monetary union than does
Figure 6.1. Asymmetry makes monetary union less feasible (shifting
the desirable region down and the acceptable region to the right). A

larger country i makes the boundaries of the desirable region slope down more steeply, as the country has a greater influence over the monetary policy of the currency area should it join. In this parameterization, there is no part of the space where dollarisation is attractive, since the shock asymmetries are too great.

6.6. Appendix

Independent currency

$$E\left(\pi_i^I\right) = \frac{\gamma\mu b}{\Lambda} F_i + \frac{b+\gamma+\gamma\mu}{\Lambda} c, \tag{6.23}$$

$$E\left(\left(\pi_i^I\right)^2\right) = \frac{a^2(b+\gamma)^2\eta^2}{\Lambda^2}\text{var}(\varepsilon_i) + E\left(\pi_i^I\right)^2, \tag{6.24}$$

$$E\left(\pi_i^I \varepsilon_i\right) = -\frac{a(b+\gamma)\eta}{\Lambda}\text{var}(\varepsilon_i). \tag{6.25}$$

Dollarisation

$$E\left(\pi_{\overline{h}}^*\right) = \frac{\gamma\mu b}{\Lambda} F_A^{\overline{h}} + \frac{\left(1-\theta_A^{\overline{h}}\right)(b+\gamma)+\gamma\mu}{\Lambda} c, \tag{6.26}$$

$$E\left(\left(\pi_{\overline{h}}^*\right)^2\right) = \frac{a^2(b+\gamma)^2\eta^2}{\Lambda^2}\text{var}\left(\varepsilon_A^{\overline{h}}\right) + E\left(\pi_{\overline{h}}^*\right)^2, \tag{6.27}$$

$$E\left(\pi_{\overline{h}}^*\varepsilon_i\right) = -\frac{a(b+\gamma)\eta}{\Lambda}\text{cov}\left(\varepsilon_i,\varepsilon_A^{\overline{h}}\right). \tag{6.28}$$

Monetary union

$$\begin{aligned}
E\left(\pi_h^*\right) &= \frac{\gamma\mu b}{\Lambda} F_A^h + \frac{\left(1-\theta_A^h\right)(b+\gamma)+\gamma\mu}{\Lambda} c \\
&= \frac{\gamma\mu b}{\Lambda}\left(\omega_i^h F_i + (1-\omega_i^h)F_A^{\overline{h}}\right) \\
&\quad + \frac{\left[1-\left(\omega_i^h\theta_{i,h}+\left(1-\omega_i^h\right)\theta_A^{\overline{h}}\right)\right](b+\gamma)+\gamma\mu}{\Lambda} c,
\end{aligned}$$

$$\tag{6.29}$$

$$E\left((\pi_h^*)^2\right) = \frac{a^2(b+\gamma)^2\eta^2}{\Lambda^2}\text{var}\left(\varepsilon_A^h\right) + E(\pi_h^*)^2$$

$$= \frac{a^2(b+\gamma)^2\eta^2}{\Lambda^2}\left[\left(\omega_i^h\right)^2\text{var}\left(\varepsilon_i\right) + \left(1-\omega_i^h\right)^2\text{var}\left(\varepsilon_A^{\overline{h}}\right)\right.$$

$$\left. + 2\omega_i^h\left(1-\omega_i^h\right)\text{cov}\left(\varepsilon_i, \varepsilon_A^{\overline{h}}\right)\right] + E(\pi_h^*)^2, \qquad (6.30)$$

$$E\left(\pi_h^*\varepsilon_i\right) = -\frac{a(b+\gamma)\eta}{\Lambda}\text{cov}\left(\varepsilon_i, \varepsilon_A^h\right)$$

$$= -\frac{a(b+\gamma)\eta}{\Lambda}\left[\omega_i^h\text{var}\left(\varepsilon_i\right) + \left(1-\omega_i^h\right)\text{cov}\left(\varepsilon_i, \varepsilon_A^{\overline{h}}\right)\right]. \qquad (6.31)$$

Net gain for country i from dollarisation

$$DN_i = \frac{1}{2\Lambda^2}\left\{a\left[\gamma\mu by + \theta_A^{\overline{h}}(b+\gamma)c\right]\left[\begin{array}{c}\gamma\mu b\left(2F_A^{\overline{h}} + y\right)\\ + \left(2 - \theta_A^{\overline{h}}\right)(b+\gamma)c + 2\gamma\mu c\end{array}\right]\right.$$

$$- a^2(b+\gamma)\eta^2\left[a(b+\gamma)\text{var}\left(\varepsilon_A^{\overline{h}}\right) + \Lambda\text{var}\left(\varepsilon_i\right)\right.$$

$$\left. - 2\Lambda\text{cov}\left(\varepsilon_A^{\overline{h}}, \varepsilon_i\right)\right] - \frac{\gamma\mu}{b+\gamma}\left[\gamma\mu b\left(F_A^{\overline{h}} + y\right) + (b+\gamma+\gamma\mu)c\right]$$

$$\left. \times \left[\begin{array}{c}b\left(2\Lambda - \gamma\mu^2 b\right)\left(F_A^{\overline{h}} + y\right)\\ + c\left(2\Lambda - \mu b(b+\gamma+\gamma\mu)\right)\end{array}\right]\right\}, \qquad (6.32)$$

Net gain for country i from monetary union

$$MU_i = -\frac{1}{2\Lambda}\left\{\left[\frac{\gamma\mu b}{b+\gamma}\left(1-\omega_i^h\right)y + \left(\theta_A^{\overline{h}} + \omega_i^h x\right)c\right]\right.$$

$$\times \left[\gamma\mu b\left(1-\omega_i^h\right)y - \left(2 - \theta_A^{\overline{h}} - \omega_i^h x\right)(b+\gamma)c\right] + a^2\eta^2(b+\gamma)$$

$$\left. \times (1-\omega_i^h)^2\left[\text{var}\left(\varepsilon_A^{\overline{h}}\right) - 2\text{cov}\left(\varepsilon_i, \varepsilon_A^{\overline{h}}\right) + \text{var}\left(\varepsilon_i\right)\right]\right\}. \qquad (6.33)$$

Net gain for median country to admit i to monetary union

$$A = -\frac{\omega_i^h}{2(b+\gamma)\Lambda} \left\{ \omega_i^h \left[\gamma\mu by - \left(b+\gamma\right)cx \right]^2 \right.$$
$$+ 2\left(1 - \theta_A^{\overline{h}}\right)\left(b+\gamma\right)c\left[\gamma\mu by - (b+\gamma)cx\right]$$
$$+ a^2\eta^2(b+\gamma)^2 \left[\omega_i^h \left(\text{var}\left(\varepsilon_i\right) - 2\text{cov}\left(\varepsilon_i, \varepsilon_A^{\overline{h}}\right) + \text{var}\left(\varepsilon_A^{\overline{h}}\right) \right) \right.$$
$$\left. \left. + 2\left(\text{cov}\left(\varepsilon_i, \varepsilon_A^{\overline{h}}\right) + \text{cov}\left(\varepsilon_j, \varepsilon_A^{\overline{h}}\right) - \text{cov}\left(\varepsilon_i, \varepsilon_j\right) - \text{var}\left(\varepsilon_A^{\overline{h}}\right) \right) \right] \right\}.$$

$$(6.34)$$

Chapter 7

Monetary Union with an Independent Central Bank

7.1. Monetary Policy Independence

In the previous chapter, we considered a dependent central bank — one that shared the objectives of the government, and, in particular, had the same target for government expenditure and hence employed inflation as a way of generating revenues for the government in order to finance that expenditure. In this chapter, we will make a different assumption concerning the central bank, namely that it is able to pursue different objectives from those of the government. Typically, an institutional set-up that granted independence to the central bank would also give it the responsibility to target specific objectives that would usually include price stability. Although it might also value higher output, it would not place an explicit utility weight on government expenditure, and hence would not want to generate seigniorage as a source of financing. However, such a central bank might not be completely free from pressures from the government. The reason that this might occur, as we shall see below, is that absent central bank financing the government would have to impose taxes, which would have a negative effect on output. Provided the central bank included output in its objective function, it could therefore be influenced indirectly to provide financing if the fiscal authorities acted first.

Another aspect to the question is whether each country chooses its fiscal policy independently, or, instead, fiscal policy among the members of a monetary union is coordinated. Recall that in the model of a dependent central bank, the influence of each government on the central bank's financing via inflation is diluted by the fact that it is only one of n countries in the union. The same holds true for the case of an independent central bank that is nevertheless indirectly induced to provide financing. Policy coordination among the fiscal authorities can reverse this dilution effect, because if they have the same interest in extracting more seigniorage, then by getting together they can exert the same pressure on the central bank as would a single government facing a single central bank.

In sum, central bank "independence" does not imply that the bank is free to ignore what the fiscal authorities are doing. On the contrary, since each affects the other's ability to hit its targets, monetary–fiscal interaction remains complicated, even if the central bank is independent in the sense of having its own objectives (either set by itself or by the government) and the instruments to pursue them. If it has more targets than instruments, then the central bank will necessarily face a trade-off between the targets, and the fiscal authorities can affect that trade-off.

7.2. A Model of an Independent Central Bank

In this chapter, we will modify the model of the previous chapter in order to revert to the more standard quadratic form of the objective function. While the specification of the previous chapter, which was linear in output (while being quadratic in inflation, taxes, and government spending), was convenient, it does not allow the interactions between the monetary and fiscal authorities that we want to model here. In particular, we will assume here that the independent central bank has a different utility function from that of the government: it does not value government spending, though it cares about output as well as inflation. The government can influence the monetary authorities through the effect of its taxes on output, but if output entered the central bank's objective function linearly, then taxes would not modify the first-order condition that determines its optimal inflation. Restoring a quadratic term in output makes the two policies — taxes and inflation — interdependent.

7.2.1. *The objective functions*

Here, both the government and the central bank want to minimise deviations around the same target for output, but the monetary authorities (superscript M) target inflation and the fiscal authorities (indicated by a superscript F) target government spending. The targets for inflation, output, and government spending are all assumed constant, but they may differ across countries. The quadratic term in output ensures that there is a stabilisation role for policy in offsetting shocks, making unnecessary the assumption of the previous chapter that the inflation target depends on the shock.

$$U_i^F = -\frac{1}{2}\{(y_i - \widetilde{y}_i)^2 + b(g_i - \widetilde{g}_i)^2\},$$
$$U_i^M = -\frac{1}{2}\{a(\pi_i - \widetilde{\pi}_i)^2 + (y_i - \widetilde{y}_i)^2\}. \tag{7.1}$$

We will further assume that neither the monetary nor the fiscal authorities fully reflects society's preferences, which are assumed to be given by

$$U_i^S = -\frac{1}{2}\{a(\pi_i - \widetilde{\pi}_i)^2 + (y_i - \widetilde{y}_i)^2 + b(g_i - \widetilde{g}_i)^2\}. \tag{7.2}$$

The rest of the model is assumed to be the same. We repeat the equations here for convenience. The supply equation is

$$y_i = c(\pi_i - \pi_i^e - \tau_i) - \sum_{k=1}^{n} \theta_{i,k} c(\pi_k - \pi_k^e) + \varepsilon_i, \quad i = 1, \ldots, n. \quad (7.3)$$

The government finances itself as before by seigniorage ($\phi_i = 1$) and taxes, while the diversion of funds means that the deviation of government spending from target can be written

$$g_i - \widetilde{g}_i = \mu\pi_i + \tau_i - F_i, \quad (7.4)$$

where F_i is the government financing need, which is the sum of the government spending target ($\widetilde{g}_i$) and non-profitable spending/tax diversion (δ_i).

7.2.2. *Independent currencies*

We first consider the case of a single fiscal authority facing a single central bank. Unlike the case of the previous chapter, in which the monetary and fiscal authorities jointly maximised the same objective function, here they act separately. Thus, it is important to define who acts first. We can distinguish a **Nash equilibrium**, where each of them takes the other's policies as given, from a **Stackelberg equilibrium**, where one of the two acts first and can anticipate the reaction of the other to its own policy settings. We will assume that the fiscal authorities act first in this case, in accordance with much of the literature.

Nash equilibrium

Here, we simply calculate the first-order conditions from maximising U_i^F with respect to τ_i and U_i^M with respect to π_i. Each takes the private expectations as given; thus this is the **discretionary**, not the **precommitment** equilibrium. We will then solve for the rational expectations of inflation. Solving the first-order conditions yields two reaction functions (see Chapter 4) so that M reacts to

F's setting of τ_i in determining π_i, and vice versa. The intersection of the two reaction functions (calculated algebraically by solving the two equations together) then yields the Nash equilibrium.

The first-order conditions can be easily calculated:

$$\frac{\partial U_i^F}{\partial \tau_i} = -\{(y_i - \widetilde{y}_i)(-c) + b(g_i - \widetilde{g}_i)\} = 0, \qquad (7.5)$$

$$\frac{\partial U_i^M}{\partial \pi_i} = -\{a(\pi_i - \widetilde{\pi}_i) + (y_i - \widetilde{y}_i)c\} = 0. \qquad (7.6)$$

Substitution for y_i and g_i then yields the reaction functions for the fiscal and monetary authorities, respectively:

$$\tau_i = \frac{1}{b + c^2}\{(c^2 - b\mu)\pi_i - c^2\pi_i^e - c(cG_i - \varepsilon_i) + bF_i - c\widetilde{y}_i\}, \quad (7.7)$$

$$\pi_i = \frac{1}{a + c^2}\{c^2\tau_i + a\widetilde{\pi}_i + c^2\pi_i^e + c(cG_i - \varepsilon_i) + c\widetilde{y}_i\}, \qquad (7.8)$$

where $G_i \equiv \sum_{k=1}^{n} \theta_{i,k}(\pi_k - \pi_k^e)$. Solving the two reaction functions together gives two semi-reduced forms:

$$\tau_i = \frac{1}{\Delta + bc^2}\{-(a + b\mu)[c^2\pi_i^e + c(cG_i - \varepsilon_i) + c\widetilde{y}_i] \\ + (a + c^2)bF_i + a(c^2 - b\mu)\widetilde{\pi}_i\},$$

$$\pi_i = \frac{1}{\Delta + bc^2}\{a(b + c^2)\widetilde{\pi}_i + bc^2\pi_i^e + bc(cG_i - \varepsilon_i) + bc\widetilde{y}_i + bc^2 F_i\},$$

where $d \equiv a + \mu c^2$ and $\Delta \equiv ac^2 + bd$.

We then take expectations of inflation, yeilding

$$\pi_i^e = \frac{1}{\Delta}\{a(b + c^2)\widetilde{\pi}_i + bc\widetilde{y}_i + bc^2 F_i\}.$$

Substituting back into the semi-reduced forms, and solving for the Nash equilibrium:

$$\tau_i = \frac{1}{\Delta}\{-ab\mu\widetilde{\pi}_i - (a + b\mu)c\widetilde{y}_i + abF_i\} - \frac{a + b\mu}{\Delta + bc^2}c(cG_i - \varepsilon_i),$$
$$(7.9)$$

$$\pi_i = \frac{1}{\Delta}\{a(b + c^2)\widetilde{\pi}_i + bc\widetilde{y}_i + bc^2 F_i\} + \frac{bc}{\Delta + bc^2}(cG_i - \varepsilon_i).$$
$$(7.10)$$

Stackelberg equilibrium

In this case, the fiscal authorities are assumed to act first, but after expectations are formed and the shock is observed (a useful alternative case would make them act before the shock was observed, which would preclude them from undertaking any stabilisation policy, that is, cushioning the effect of output shocks on the economy). In the Stackelberg case, the first-order conditions differ from the Nash, because now the fiscal authorities can take into account the induced reaction of tax setting on the monetary authorities' rate of inflation as well as on inflation expectations. Here

$$\frac{\partial U_i^F}{\partial \tau_i} = -\left\{ (y_i - \tilde{y}_i)(-c) + b(g_i - \tilde{g}_i)\left(1 + \mu\frac{\partial \pi_i}{\partial \tau_i}\right) \right\} = 0. \quad (7.11)$$

In calculating the effects on the government budget constraint of higher taxes, the fiscal authorities take into account the reaction of the monetary authorities in setting inflation. The latter are also assumed to take into account the possible effect of fiscal policy on exchange rate expectations, so we need to evaluate the derivative $\frac{\partial \pi_i}{\partial \tau_i}$ subject to $\partial \pi_i = \partial \pi_i^e$. The central bank's reaction function is unchanged from its previous specification [Equation (7.8)], giving the following partial derivative:

$$\frac{\partial \pi_i}{\partial \tau_i} = \frac{1}{a + c^2}\left\{ c^2 + c^2\frac{\partial \pi_i^e}{\partial \tau_i} \right\},$$

yielding when $\partial \pi_i = \partial \pi_i^e$

$$\frac{\partial \pi_i}{\partial \tau_i} = \frac{c^2}{a}.$$

The central bank raises inflation in response to higher taxes, in order to neutralise negative effects on output. The fiscal authorities, knowing this, can rely on the monetary authorities to respond and provide some of the financing of government expenditure. Note that the first term of (7.11) does not change relative to (7.5), however, since (rational) expectations incorporate this effect into π_i^e, and therefore $\partial(\pi_i - \pi_i^e)/\partial\tau_i = 0$.

The two reaction functions are thus

$$\tau_i = \frac{1}{\Delta}\{(ac^2 - b\mu d)\pi_i - ac^2\pi_i^e - ac(cG_i - \varepsilon_i) + bdF_i - ac\widetilde{y}_i\},$$

$$\pi_i = \frac{1}{a + c^2}\{c^2\tau_i + a\widetilde{\pi}_i + c^2\pi_i^e + c(cG_i - \varepsilon_i) + c\widetilde{y}_i\}.$$

Solving the reaction functions together gives semi-reduced-form equations for taxes and inflation that depend on inflation expectations, foreign monetary surprises, targets for inflation and output, financing needs, and the shock to output. We report only the equation for inflation, the variable of interest:

$$\pi_i = \frac{1}{\Omega}\{bd[c^2\pi_i^e + c(cG_i - \varepsilon_i) + c\widetilde{y}_i] + bc^2dF_i + a\Delta\widetilde{\pi}_i\},$$

where $\Omega \equiv (a^2 + bd)c^2 + bd^2$.

We then proceed by taking expectations, yielding

$$\pi_i^e = \frac{1}{bd^2 + a^2c^2}\{bcd\widetilde{y}_i + bc^2dF_i + a\Delta\widetilde{\pi}_i\}.$$

Substituting this result back into the expression for inflation yields the Stackelberg equilibrium:

$$\pi_i = \frac{1}{bd^2 + a^2c^2}[bcd\widetilde{y}_i + bc^2dF_i + a\Delta\widetilde{\pi}_i] + \frac{bcd}{\Omega}(cG_i - \varepsilon_i). \quad (7.12)$$

While (7.12) is complicated, first note that even if $\widetilde{\pi}_i = 0$ and $\varepsilon_i = G_i = 0$, $\pi_i > 0$, because $\widetilde{y}_i, F_i > 0$. This is true also of the Nash equilibrium for inflation, Equation (7.9). Thus, if the zero target reflects society's preferences as well, but society valued government spending with the same weight as the fiscal authorities, then the Pareto optimal policy would be to use just enough inflation to finance government spending, but not to try to stimulate output. This outcome could be achieved if precommitment by the central bank were possible. The solution can be found by maximising the welfare function with respect to expected inflation as well as actual inflation (with the constraint that *ex ante* they were the same).

Comparison of Equations (7.9) and (7.12) shows that the Stackelberg equilibrium for inflation responds more strongly to output shocks than does the Nash, since the fiscal policy authorities internalise the monetary reaction function in their optimisation. In addition, the inflation rate responds more strongly to the government's financing requirement. We will assert without proof that, as in the standard Barro–Gordon model, the Pareto optimal solution yields lower inflation than either the Nash or the Stackelberg equilibrium. We will also leave as an exercise for the reader to compare the level of inflation in the Nash and Stackelberg equilibria.

7.2.3. *Monetary union with fiscal authorities acting first*

In this case, the common central bank faces not a single fiscal authority but several. This fundamentally changes the nature of monetary–fiscal interactions, and we will show that it reduces the inflationary bias from the Stackelberg equilibrium. Here, the monetary authority maximises a weighted average of objective functions U_i^M (7.1). For convenience, we will assume that there are n equally sized countries in the monetary union, and that all trade by the same amount $\overline{\theta}$ with each of the others so $\theta_A = (n-1)\overline{\theta}$. Moreover, we will assume that the monetary union comprises the whole world, so H is the null set. So the central bank maximises with respect to inflation

$$U^{MU} = -\frac{1}{2}\frac{1}{n}\sum_{i=1}^{n}\{a(\pi - \widetilde{\pi})^2 + (y_i - \widetilde{y}_i)^2\},$$

where

$$y_i = c(\pi - \pi^e)\left(1 - \sum_{k=1}^{n}\theta_{i,k}\right) - c\tau_i + \varepsilon_i$$
$$= c(\pi - \pi^e)(1 - \theta_A) - c\tau_i + \varepsilon_i, \quad i = 1,\ldots,n.$$

The first-order condition now can be written as

$$\frac{\partial U^{MU}}{\partial \pi} = a(\pi - \tilde{\pi}) + \frac{1}{n}\sum_{i=1}^{n}(y_i - \tilde{y}_i)c\,(1 - \theta_A) = 0.$$

Using (as in the previous chapter) a subscript A to denote the average across the n countries, after substituting for each country's output equation the FOC becomes

$$a(\pi - \tilde{\pi}) + [c(1 - \theta_A)(\pi - \pi^e) - c\tau_A + \varepsilon_A - \tilde{y}_A]c\,(1 - \theta_A) = 0,$$

where, as in the previous chapter, the parameter θ_A reflects the fact that the monetary union internalises inflation spillovers and hence removes the temptation to increase inflation in order to stimulate output at the expense of neighbouring countries. As in the case of a single fiscal authority facing a single central bank, the fiscal authorities are assumed to act first, giving them a strategic advantage over the central bank. The central bank's reaction function is derived from its FOC, yielding

$$\pi = \frac{1}{a + c^2\,(1 - \theta_A)^2}\{c^2\,(1 - \theta_A)\,\tau_A + a\tilde{\pi} + c^2\,(1 - \theta_A)^2$$
$$\times \pi^e - c\,(1 - \theta_A)\,\varepsilon_A + c\,(1 - \theta_A)\,\tilde{y}_A\} \tag{7.13}$$

Each individual country's fiscal policy reaction function is unchanged from before, except that it now faces a single monetary authority, and individually it has only $1/n$th the weight it had before on monetary policy, since $\partial \tau_A / \partial \tau_i = 1/n$. Taking the derivative of (7.13) with respect to τ_i, taking into account the changes in expectations as before:

$$\frac{\partial \pi}{\partial \tau_i} = \frac{c^2\,(1 - \theta_A)\,/n}{a}.$$

Maximising utility, taking into account the induced change in monetary policy, the FOC for each fiscal authority is again

$$\frac{\partial U_i^F}{\partial \tau_i} = -\left\{(y_i - \tilde{y}_i)(-c) + b(g_i - \tilde{g}_i)\left(1 + \mu\frac{\partial \pi}{\partial \tau_i}\right)\right\} = 0,$$

yielding

$$[c(\pi - \pi^e)(1 - \theta_A) - c\tau_i + \varepsilon_i - \widetilde{y}_i](-c)$$
$$+ b(g_i - \widetilde{g}_i)\left[1 + \mu\frac{c^2(1 - \theta_A)/n}{a}\right] = 0.$$

Solving for each country's reaction function and then aggregating by averaging over the n countries, give an aggregate tax reaction function:

$$\tau_A = \frac{1}{\Gamma}\{[ac^2(1 - \theta_A) - b\mu e]\pi$$
$$- ac^2(1 - \theta_A)\pi^e + ac(\varepsilon_A - \widetilde{y}_A) + beF_A\}, \qquad (7.14)$$

where $e \equiv a + c^2\mu(1 - \theta_A)/n$ and $\Gamma \equiv ac^2 + be$.

The resulting semi-reduced-form equation for inflation is given by

$$\pi = \frac{1}{\Lambda}\{bc^2e(1 - \theta_A)^2\pi^e - bce(1 - \theta_A)\varepsilon_A$$
$$+ bce(1 - \theta_A)\widetilde{y}_A + bc^2e(1 - \theta_A)F_A + a\Gamma\widetilde{\pi}\},$$

where $\Lambda \equiv a\Gamma + bc^2e(1 - \theta_A)[\mu + (1 - \theta_A)]$.

After taking expectations and substituting back, the Stackelberg equilibrium for inflation is found to be

$$\pi = \frac{1}{\Sigma}\{a\Gamma\widetilde{\pi} + bce(1 - \theta_A)\widetilde{y}_A + bc^2e(1 - \theta_A)F_A]\}$$
$$- \frac{bce(1 - \theta_A)}{\Lambda}\varepsilon_A, \qquad (7.15)$$

where now $\Sigma \equiv \Lambda - bc^2e(1 - \theta_A)^2$.

As compared to the situation of a single fiscal authority and central bank, now the strategic advantage of each government is diluted. With reference to (7.11), the impact of any government's tax setting on the common inflation rate goes to zero as the number of countries goes to infinity, and this means that $e \to a$. The result is to reduce the effect on the coefficient of F_A in (7.15) — though not necessarily to the Nash equilibrium level. However, given that the inflation rate is too high from the society's point of view, forming a monetary union is welfare improving (leaving aside the asymmetry of shocks) since it will reduce the inflationary bias — both because $\theta_A > 0$ and because μ/n declines.

7.2.4. *Fiscal policy coordination*

A counterexample to the assertion that monetary union reduces the strategic advantage for the fiscal authorities in the context of a Stackelberg equilibrium concerns the possibility of coordination of fiscal policies [see Beetsma and Bovenberg (1998)]. The intuition is straightforward. Here, assume that the fiscal authorities jointly maximise a weighted average of their objective functions. By taking into account the influence that higher inflation has on all the other countries' budget revenues, the fiscal authorities reestablish their strategic advantage. Thus, the equilibrium resembles the one described above, between a single fiscal authority that acts first and a single central bank (though monetary union still reduces the temptation for monetary stimulus, and thus reduces the inflationary bias).

While we will not go through this case in detail, it is useful to write down the optimisation problem of the fiscal authorities. Acting jointly, they will choose $\tau_1, \tau_2, \ldots, \tau_n$ to maximise the sum of the national objective functions

$$U^F = -\frac{1}{2}\sum\{(y_i - \widetilde{y}_i)^2 + b(g_i - \widetilde{g}_i)^2\}.$$

Note that we are not assuming that there is a single fiscal policy; instead, the optimal policy allows each country's tax rate to reflect its own variables $\widetilde{y}_i$, F_i, and ε_i.

If we look at a typical first-order condition, for instance, for τ_j, it can be written as

$$[c(1 - \theta_A)(\pi - \pi^e) - c\tau_j + \varepsilon_j - \widetilde{y}_j]c - b\sum_{i=1}^{n}(g_i - \widetilde{g}_i)\mu\frac{\partial\pi}{\partial\tau_j}$$

$$- b[\mu\pi + \tau_j - F_j] = 0. \tag{7.16}$$

Note that the increase in inflation impacts all countries' budget constraints (the middle term), thus magnifying its impact in the optimisation decision, but taxes only raise the own country's revenues directly (the last term). Equation (7.16) can be averaged over all countries, and the resulting reaction function for τ_A can be written

$$\tau_A = \frac{1}{\Gamma} \left\{ \begin{array}{c} [ac^2(1 - \theta_A) - b\mu(a + c^2\mu(1 - \theta_A))]\pi - ac^2(1 - \theta_A)\pi^e \\ + ac(\varepsilon_A - \tilde{y}_A) + b[a + c^2\mu(1 - \theta_A)]F_A \end{array} \right\},$$

(7.17)

where $\Gamma \equiv ac^2 + b[a + c^2\mu(1 - \theta_A)]$. Comparison of (7.17) with (7.14) shows that the diluting effect of having many fiscal authorities disappears, since it equals the earlier expression with e evaluated at $n = 1$. Fiscal policy reestablishes its full strategic advantage over monetary policy, as in the Stackelberg example for a single fiscal authority facing a single central bank discussed earlier (though there are still n different fiscal policies facing the single central bank).

7.2.5. *Alternative institutional arrangements*

One can get closer to the best outcome by changing the target assigned to the central bank. As in the case of a single economy, in a monetary union one can improve welfare by delegating monetary policy to a central bank that has different preferences from society's. In general, this will mean putting a greater weight than society's on inflation, since doing so will help to counteract fiscal policy's strategic advantage. Another monetary delegation arrangement would involve giving to the common central bank a lower inflation target than the level desired by society (in our set-up the inflation target would be less than zero).

Given the distorting effects of fiscal policy on monetary policy, it is natural to consider constraints on the fiscal authorities. Indeed, this is the rationale in the European context for the Stability and Growth Pact (SGP), which constrains fiscal deficits and the public debt. In an extension to the model presented one can show that a monetary union may exacerbate tendencies of governments to incur excessive debt (for instance, because their discount rates are higher than society's, due to electoral cycles). Since the costs of higher inflation are borne by all countries, countries (and indeed, their fiscal authorities) may be willing to accept limits on their indebtedness as part of being in a monetary union, though they would not have been willing to do so in the case of independent currencies. Thus the externality may justify the additional constraints imposed. This provides a convincing rationale for the SGP, though the unrealistic assumption of identical countries seems necessary to justify the imposition of a uniform ceiling on debt (60 percent of GDP) or deficits (3 percent of GDP). Beetsma and Debrun (2004) provide a survey of the theoretical literature on the SGP.

Part IV

Sovereign Debt

Chapter 8

Why do Sovereigns Repay Their Debts?

8.1. Background

Though there were earlier episodes of default on sovereign debt, that
is, the bonds and bank borrowing of sovereign countries' governments — in particular, in the late 19th century and in the 1930s —
the analytical literature mainly dates back to the 1980s when a
default by Mexico in August 1982 led to a generalised third-world
debt crisis (see Box 8.1 for more details). The 1970s and early 1980s
saw extensive recycling of "petrodollars" (the earnings of OPEC
countries) through international banks to various developing country borrowers — often without a great deal of attention paid to the
profitability of investments or the uses to which the funds would be
put. The decision by Mexico not to service its debts reminded lenders
that sovereign borrowers were different from commercial borrowers in
advanced countries, where there are extensive legal provisions that

facilitate debt collection and, in case of bankruptcy, legal protection for borrowers and court procedures for restructuring/liquidation (e.g., Chapter 11 in the United States). None of these avenues for recourse is available to international lenders; countries cannot be liquidated and the possibility of seizing assets of defaulted countries is limited — though not impossible.

Box 8.1. Background to the 1980s Third-World Debt Crisis

- 1973–1974 and 1979–1980. Oil price increases boost oil-exporting countries' assets. These "petrodollars" are largely placed with international banks, which, faced with weak investment demand in the industrial countries, on-lend them to developing countries at low rates of interest. Credit quality is not scrutinised, in line with Citicorp chairman Walter Wriston's dictum that "countries don't go bankrupt". Loans are typically at floating rate and in US dollars, so are sensitive to movements in short-term US rates.
- 1979–1982. Concern with US inflation leads the Federal Reserve to adopt a sharply restrictive monetary policy, raising US short rates and thus also interest rates on developing countries' outstanding loans.
- 1980–1986. Fall in commodity prices depresses the export receipts of many developing countries.
- 1982. Oil prices fall, hurting Mexico's exports and the government's revenue; the fiscal deficit widens to over 10 percent of GDP. In August, Mexico declares it cannot service its outstanding debts. The changeover between outgoing president Lopez Portillo and incoming president De la Madrid complicates decisions on policy reforms and resolution of the crisis. Bankers soon attempt to reduce their exposure to most developing countries, and absence of financing makes many of them in turn unable to service outstanding debts.

(Continued)

Box 8.1. (*Continued*)

- 1982–1989. The IMF provides financing to countries willing to make structural adjustments that will improve their creditworthiness; at the same time, along with industrial country authorities, it puts pressure on banks to continue lending ("concerted lending") or to reschedule outstanding loans by extending their maturity. Developing countries however continue to be forced to run current account surpluses to finance the outflows of capital, and this is accompanied by slow or negative growth, leading to the use of the term "lost decade" to characterise the 1980s.
- 1985. The Baker Plan (named after the US Treasury Secretary) provides for new disbursements by international financial institutions (principally the IMF and the World Bank) and by commercial banks to countries willing to make serious efforts to adjust their policies. In practice, banks resist the provision of new money since they are still trying to disengage from international lending.
- 1987. Banks start to work out new agreements with debtor countries that include debt relief or reduction.
- 1989. Brady Plan (named once again for the incumbent US Treasury Secretary) calls for voluntary debt reduction in exchange for new collateralised debt, with the IMF now allowed to "lend into arrears," i.e., to countries that do not have agreements with their creditors. The Brady bonds, which are traded on financial markets, facilitate disengagement by banks from developing country exposure and the elimination in developing countries of "debt overhangs" that are by now widely viewed as inimical to needed investment and growth.
- 1990. Portfolio investment surges to developing countries, marking an end to the debt crisis.

Source: James (1996).

The debt crisis led to a theoretical literature on whether it was rational for lenders to lend under these circumstances — had the lending boom just been a big mistake? What was it that permitted any lending to take place, since lenders could not be sure that there were incentives for repayment or means to coerce them to do so? Even if the lending regime supported a positive value of debt, was this level optimal? In the presence of negative shocks, it was obvious that restructuring of the debt might prove necessary, and many articles considered the issue of negotiations between lenders and defaulted debtors.

The literature also considered how the multiplicity of lenders (with imperfect information) might interact occasionally to produce excessive lending, and how this multiplicity might be associated with collective action problems which would impede a settlement if the borrower could not pay. The end of the 1980s saw a series of restructuring deals that replaced bank debt by bonds ("Brady bonds") that were designed to allow banks to exit from third-world lending — though these deals involved "haircuts", that is, reduction of principal, interest, or both.

Table 8.1 gives a summary of the sources of financing flows to developing countries, and their breakdown by recipient region. Four things can be noted from these data, which extend from the Mexican "tequila crisis" of 1994–1995 through the Asian currency crises and Argentina's default on over $100 billion of debt in 2001. First, direct investment is a substantial and stable source of flows; in recent years, it is the largest among the categories; portfolio equity flows are relatively modest in all years. Second, debt flows — predominantly loans from banks and non-official lenders to sovereign borrowers — were a very large source of financing in the mid-1990s but have diminished greatly since. Third, debt flows are very volatile. We can see in the data the sharp reduction in lending to East Asia brought on by the 1997 crisis, as the inflow of $45 billion in 1997 turned into an outflow of $33 billion in 1998. Since then, though Europe and Central Asia have received continuing large debt inflows, other regions have not. Finally, the distribution of financing — in total and by type of

Table 8.1. External financing of developing countries (in billions of US dollars).

Region	1995	1996	1997	1998	1999	2000	2001	2002	2003
Net inward foreign direct investment									
East Asia and Pacific	51	59	62	58	50	44	48	55	57
Europe and Central Asia	17	16	23	26	28	29	32	33	26
Latin America and Carib.	31	44	67	74	88	77	70	45	37
Middle East and N. Afr.	−1	1	6	7	3	2	6	3	2
South Asia	3	4	5	4	3	3	5	4	5
Sub-Saharan Africa	4	4	8	7	9	6	14	8	9
All developing	105	128	171	176	181	161	175	148	136
Net inward portfolio equity flows									
East Asia and Pacific	6	10	−4	−3	2	5	1	4	5
Europe and Central Asia	2	4	4	4	2	1	0	0	1
Latin America and Carib.	5	12	13	−2	−4	−1	2	2	1
Middle East and N. Afr.	0	0	1	0	1	0	0	0	0
South Asia	2	4	3	−1	2	3	2	1	7
Sub-Saharan Africa	3	2	6	9	9	4	−1	0	1
All developing	18	32	23	7	12	12	4	7	15
Net inward debt flows									
East Asia and Pacific	54	52	45	−33	−12	−18	−8	−11	1
Europe and Central Asia	23	23	33	42	16	21	2	25	30
Latin America and Carib.	61	37	25	38	12	−10	6	−8	20
Middle East and N. Afr.	2	−1	−3	7	−2	−6	1	1	−8
South Asia	3	3	1	5	1	3	−1	0	−2
Sub-Saharan Africa	8	3	4	−1	−1	−1	−2	0	5
All developing	151	117	105	58	14	−11	−2	7	46

Source: World Bank, Global Development Finance, 2004; figures do not add to totals there due to rounding.

flow — varies greatly across regions. East Asia and the Pacific receive the largest amount of direct investment, and much of that goes to China. Sub-Saharan Africa receives little equity or debt financing, and much of this goes to South Africa, not to the poorest countries that make up much of the rest of the continent. Their financing, modest as it is, takes the form mainly of official financing. In recent years, recorded official financing has been boosted by one-time debt write-offs by rich country governments, the World Bank, and the IMF.

The volatility of debt flows (especially short-term debt) has led some critics to argue that foreign borrowing should be limited, because outstanding debt provides a potential trigger for a balance of payments crisis. Guillermo Calvo, for instance, has noted that developing countries suffer from "sudden stops" in their debt finance, which may be triggered by objective circumstances, contagion effects from other countries, or from global liquidity conditions. Countries that have a large amount of debt maturing in a short period are especially vulnerable to a reversal of investor sentiment. If they cannot obtain new loans to roll over maturing debt, then the capital account may have to go into large deficit as the countries repay their debt, and, in the absence of foreign exchange reserves that can be drawn down, they must generate a large current account surplus. In this case, borrowing countries are forced either to contract demand sharply in order to restrict imports or to experience a sharp currency depreciation to make exports more competitive (and imports dearer), or both. The alternative is to default on their debt — but this alternative is itself likely to reinforce the unwillingness of investors to extend new lending for some time into the future. The need to generate a current account surplus provides a link between debt crises (sudden stops) and currency crises, studied in Part I of this book.

Most of the lending to developing countries is denominated not in the borrowing country's currency, but rather in one of the major international currencies — principally in US dollars. Thus, the interest rate on their borrowing does not reflect the considerations embodied in the interest rate parity conditions of Chapter 1, where the domestic interest rate (that is, on claims denominated in the local currency) was higher than the foreign rate when there were fears that the currency would be devalued. Instead, the interest rate charged to developing countries on their foreign borrowing in US dollars reflects fears that the borrower would default on that debt rather than fears of devaluation. However, the two relationships are in fact very similar. Indeed, if π is the probability of a default over the relevant period, and investors expect to receive nothing in the case of a default, then risk-neutral investors would equate expected returns on domestic debt i with the risk-free foreign rate i^*:

$$(1 - \pi)(1 + i) = 1 + i^*.$$

Compare this expression with Equation (1.5).

Thus, interest rates charged to developing country borrowers reflect the factors that may help to predict a default, and that are negatively associated with their ability and willingness to repay their debts. Thus, during the Asian currency crises, the interest rates charged on their foreign borrowing rose greatly, as capital flowed out of these countries and output contracted. Moreover, the same phenomenon of contagion shows up in the dollar interest rates that they pay, which have tended to rise when other countries in the region are facing difficulties. Charts 8.1–8.4 plot the **spreads** over US treasury securities (that is, $i - i^*$) charged to selected developing country borrowers during four crisis periods: the Mexican crisis of 1994–1995, the Asian crisis of 1997–1998, the Russian default of August 1998, and Argentina's default in 2001. We can see the Asian crisis especially showed a very sharp rise in all interest rate spreads, which came down again when the crisis receded. In contrast, Argentina's default was viewed as specific to that country, and it provoked little impact on other countries' borrowing costs. Indeed, despite the

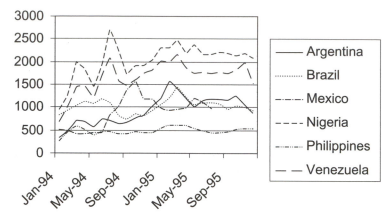

Chart 8.1. Emerging market spreads, Mexico crisis.
Source: JP Morgan.

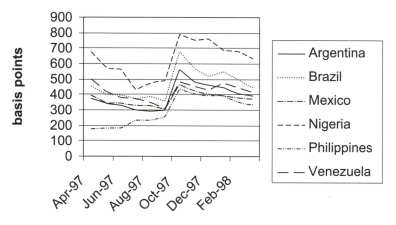

Chart 8.2. Emerging market spreads, Asian crisis.
Source: JP Morgan.

record size of Argentina's default, developing country spreads have
narrowed substantially in the last four years, and are at historic lows.
The reasons for Argentina's crisis have been the subject of many
studies [see, among others IMF (2004) and Mussa (2002)]. The currency board linking the peso one-to-one to the US dollar was an

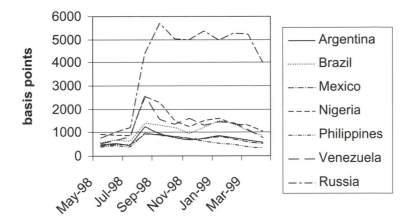

Chart 8.3. Emerging market spreads, Russian crisis.
Source: JP Morgan.

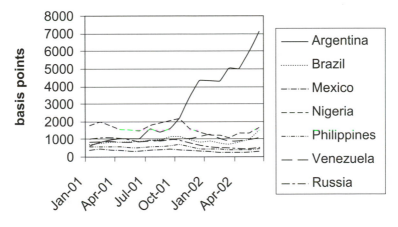

Chart 8.4. Emerging market spreads, Argentina crisis.
Source: JP Morgan.

important factor inhibiting the growth in that country that would
have been required to make servicing the foreign debt sustainable. A
chronology of the events leading up to Argentina's default is given
in Box 8.2.

Box 8.2. A Selective Chronology of Events Associated with Argentina's 2001 Default

- 1991. Argentina under the leadership of President Carlos Menem and Finance Minister Domingo Cavallo approves the Convertibility Law, which fixes parity of the currency to the US dollar.
- 1992. The IMF approves the first of a series of programs with Argentina, endorsing its policies and providing financing.
- 1994. Mercosur is created comprising Argentina, Brazil, Paraguay, and Uruguay as a vehicle for regional integration and trade liberalisation.
- 1995–1996. Argentina weathers the effects of Mexico's "tequila crisis", which raises interest rates on Argentina's external debt. Argentina strengthens supervision of banking system and arranges an emergency line of credit from international (commercial) banks.
- 1996. Cavallo resigns as minister because Congress does not approve fiscal adjustment package.
- 1998–1999. President Menem attempts to change constitution in order to be allowed to run a third time. Economic policy is stalled amid manoeuvring between central government and provinces. The economy enters a long recession.
- January 1999. Brazil floats its currency, allowing the *real* to depreciate, which adversely affects Argentina's external competitiveness, but the parity with the US dollar prevents any similar adjustment of the Argentine peso.
- December 1999. Fernando De La Ruà takes office as president.
- March 2001. Domingo Cavallo is appointed Minister of Economy. He announces the following month a modification of the Convertibility Law, with the replacement of the dollar by an equally weighted basket of the dollar and euro (to take effect when the two reach parity).
- June 2001. Argentina completes a "mega swap" of outstanding debt, extending maturities but increasing interest costs.

(Continued)

Box 8.2. (*Continued*)

- July 2001. A zero-deficit plan is announced that is to bring expenditures in line with revenues.
- August 2001. The IMF announces an augmentation of the financing extended to Argentina, approved the following month.
- November 2001. Argentina declared in "selective default" of its external debt by Standard and Poor's.
- December 2001. Minister Cavallo and President De La Ruà resign. Three interim presidents take office briefly, until Eduardo Duhalde is elected by the Legislative Assembly to serve as President until 2003.
- January 2002. Duhalde announces the end of Convertibility, leading to an immediate depreciation of the peso, which goes from 1:1 to 4 to the dollar two months later. Different exchange rates are used to convert bank assets and liabilities. Capital controls are imposed.
- May 2003. Nestor Kirchner takes over as president and becomes popular for his defiant stance vis-à-vis foreign creditors and the IMF.
- March 2005. Final settlement is reached with 76 percent of foreign creditors, reimbursing them around 30 cents for each dollar of debt. Holdouts continue their fight to get full reimbursement.
- December 2005. Argentina announces its intention to repay early its outstanding debts to the IMF, in full; it does so in January 2006, with the help of a loan from Venezuela.

Sources: IMF (2004), and press reports.

8.2.   Deterministic Income Fluctuations

A key insight from the literature on sovereign debt [see Eaton and Gersovitz (1981) and Eaton and Fernandez (1995)] is that absent any punishment that can be imposed on the borrower (or the ability to provide a convincing precommitment that the latter will repay), then at any point in time, the discounted present value of repayment obligations must be no greater than the benefits from continuing to repay (that is, the costs of default). Working this out analytically is insightful.

It is assumed that borrowing is to smooth consumption in the face of fluctuating income. The country faces a constant gross world interest rate (actually, one plus the usual interest rate) $r > 1$, and a discount factor $\beta < 1/r$. Note that this gives a potentially unlimited demand on the part of the country to borrow on world capital markets if it does not pay a risk premium. The country's utility function is

$$U_t = \sum_{\tau=t}^{\infty} \beta^\tau u(c_\tau). \tag{8.1}$$

Output y is deterministic (but not constant), and there is no storage technology; so the only way to do consumption smoothing is through international borrowing. Debt evolves according to

$$D_{t+1} = (D_t - p_t)r = (D_t - y_t + c_t)r, \tag{8.2}$$

where p is the payment from the borrower to the creditor, which can be negative.

Consider the case where the country could precommit to repay its debt; its maximisation decision would be only limited by a single present value constraint. So

$$\max_{c_t} U = \sum_{t=0}^{\infty} \beta^t u(c_t),$$

$$\text{s.t.} \sum_{t=0}^{\infty} c_t/r^t \leq \sum_{t=0}^{\infty} y_t/r^t. \tag{8.3}$$

If the country could not borrow at all, then this maximisation would simply yield

$$c_t = y_t, \ \forall t.$$

This is the case of autarchy, and since there is no storage technology, smoothing would not be possible at all.

In contrast, with unrestricted borrowing, the optimal policy from (8.3) would yield the first-order condition

$$(r\beta)^t u'(c_t) = \lambda, \ \forall t, \tag{8.4}$$

where λ is the Lagrange multiplier for the constraint in (8.3). We can see from (8.4) that since $r\beta < 1$, marginal utility of consumption must increase as t increases along this optimal consumption path, which means monotonically decreasing consumption. The intuition behind this is that with unconstrained borrowing and a rate of time preference that exceeds the interest rate, countries want to borrow a lot now so as to raise consumption in one big step, even if that means decreasing living standards from then on. So, in effect, the borrowers would be front-end loading the benefits and paying for it later. Would lenders agree to that sort of behaviour?

To get specific analytic results it is necessary to look at a special case, as do Eaton and Fernandez. Let us assume that the country has log utility, and the output takes on only two values, y_H in odd periods and y_L in even periods (with $y_H > y_L$). Starting in period 0 (when output is low), the present value of the country's income is given by

$$V_0 = \frac{r(r y_L + y_H)}{r^2 - 1}. \tag{8.5}$$

This can be seen by expressing V_0 as follows:

$$V_0 = \sum_{t=0}^{\infty} y_t / r^t = \sum_{t=0}^{\infty} y_L / r^{2t} + \sum_{t=0}^{\infty} y_H / r^{2t+1}.$$

So, from (8.4), the precommitment solution in this case would be given by

$$(r\beta)^t / c_t^* = \lambda, \ \forall t$$

Substituting this into the intertemporal budge constraint (assuming equality), we can eliminate λ:

$$V_0 = \sum_{t=0}^{\infty} c_t/r^t = \sum_{t=0}^{\infty} \frac{(r\beta)^t}{\lambda r^t}.$$

So

$$\lambda = \frac{1}{(1-\beta)V_0},$$

and

$$c_t^* = (r\beta)^t(1-\beta)V_0. \tag{8.6}$$

As noted above, this optimal path involves monotonically declining consumption. However, there is no reason to believe that a country would have the ability to credibly precommit. So any solution to (8.3) would also have to satisfy a series of incentive compatibility constraints (one for each future period) along the consumption path. In particular, the country must not in any future period perceive greater utility from not paying (i.e., reverting to autarchy, with $c_t = y_t$, $\forall t$) than from sticking to the consumption path consistent with repaying (denoted with a tilde). These constraints are the following:

$$\sum_{\tau=t}^{\infty} \beta^\tau u(\tilde{c}_\tau) \geq \sum_{\tau=t}^{\infty} \beta^\tau u(y_\tau), \quad \forall t. \tag{8.7}$$

This is the fundamental relationship conditioning lending to sovereign debtors when precommitment is impossible and there are no other mechanisms for penalising non-payment. It implies, for instance, that there can be no period after which the country is only making non-negative repayments off until infinity (i.e., $\tilde{c}_s < y_s, \forall s$). Otherwise, the country would clearly just abandon its consumption path, default, and increase its consumption in every subsequent period. So it must be the case that only if countries expect to borrow in the future will they be willing to repay today. Thus, the desire for future access to capital markets is a necessary (but not sufficient) condition for international lending to be incentive compatible. But does it produce non-negative lending, even if not the first-best optimal given by (8.6)? We can show it does with the log utility function and for a stationary path of borrowing equal to x in low-output (even) periods and repaying rx in high-output (odd) periods. The motive is income smoothing, and positive lending is supported provided that income fluctuates enough, so that the advantages of being able to smooth outweigh the costs of servicing debt.

Note that the constraint does not bind in the (even-numbered) period of the borrowing, just the following one (when the country earns income y_H but faces the obligation to repay). We can rewrite (8.7) in this case as simply

$$\log(y_H - rx) + \beta \log(y_L + x) > \log(y_H) + \beta \log(y_L). \qquad (8.8)$$

To show that there is a solution with positive x, note that when $x = 0$ the two sides are equal, while the derivative with respect to x of the LHS is positive at $x = 0$ provided $\beta y_H > r y_L$. This is the necessary and sufficient condition for supporting positive lending in this special case. We will assume that this condition holds; it means that the output endowment in the good years must be high enough that consumption smoothing in amount x yields enough utility to compensate for the need to repay rx this period. The amount of borrowing can be found simply from maximising utility, since by construction the incentive compatibility constraints are satisfied. Utility in this case (starting in the high-output period 1) can be written as

$$U = \sum_{t=0}^{\infty} \log(y_H - rx)\beta^{2t} + \sum_{t=0}^{\infty} \log(y_L + x)\beta^{2t+1}$$

$$= \frac{1}{1 - \beta^2} [\log(y_H - rx) + \beta \log(y_L + x)].$$

Maximising utility with respect to x gives the FOC

$$\frac{\partial U}{\partial x} = \frac{1}{1 - \beta^2} \left[\frac{-r}{y_H - rx} + \frac{\beta}{y_L + x} \right] = 0,$$

which simplifies to

$$x = \frac{\beta y_H - r y_L}{r(1 + \beta)}. \tag{8.9}$$

We can show that the value of x from (8.9) is below the optimal borrowing obtained from (8.6), namely

$$x_0^* \equiv c_0^* - y_L = (1 - \beta)V_0 - y_L = \frac{(1 - \beta r^2)y_L + (1 - \beta)r y_H}{r^2 - 1},$$

provided that $\beta > r^2(\beta^2 + \beta - 1)$. Since $r^2 < 1/\beta^2$, this condition will be satisfied if $\beta^2(\beta - 1) > \beta - 1$. Since $0 < \beta < 1$, this will necessarily be true. In the optimal borrowing case, the borrower would not repay everything in the following period, but rather plan to repay over the whole of the future. The constrained level of borrowing x is also less than the amount of borrowing that would produce perfect smoothing, that is, $c_0 = c_1 = c_2 = \cdots$ which would imply $\bar{x} = (y_H - y_L)/(1 + r)$. Since $\beta r < 1$ it is the case that $x < \bar{x}$.

8.3.   Limits to Reputational Arguments

The above example motivates the argument that by not defaulting, a country acquires the reputation as a reliable borrower and retains access to international capital markets. The desire to have access in the future is, after all, a necessary condition for supporting lending in the absence of a commitment technology. But there are limits to the argument. While we will not go through the mathematics, an important limitation is that countries are assumed earlier to be unable to store from one period to another. If they can, at the world rate of interest (e.g., by acquiring riskless assets), then they can themselves do the consumption smoothing. So after borrowing (if possible) from international capital markets and acquiring assets, they would no longer have the incentive to repay.

This new set-up of course also assumes that these assets acquired to cushion future consumption are not attachable by the creditors, which is highly questionable. But if the assumption is made, then such a storage technology destroys the possibility of international lending to sovereigns, in the absence of other enforcement mechanisms.

One such mechanism, however, may be the existence of linkages between repayment history and some other relationship between creditors and debtors. Obviously countries interact in various areas, for instance international security, preferential trade access, etc. This relationship can be thought of as a trigger strategy in a supergame, and, as is well known, in infinitely repeated games, trigger strategies can sustain cooperation. Though such strategies can be imagined, they would be more convincing if it could be shown that imposing a penalty on the debtor were incentive compatible for the creditor, for instance if a default signalled some characteristic of the debtor that made it optimal for the creditor to change its strategy in the other game.

8.4. Debt Renegotiation

The experience of the 1980s showed that debt contracts were not immutable; though legally the creditors had the right to enforce the original terms, in practice with widespread defaults they were incapable of doing so. Indeed, after the original period it is useful to think of the creditor and debtor as being in a position of bilateral monopoly bargaining over repayment, without the ability to appeal definitively to any court or tribunal for a ruling on the merits of either side. In this situation, it is useful to have models that predict how settlements between them reflect the respective interests of each side.

In Eaton and Fernandez (1995, Section 2.5) this is done in the context of a "bonus" Z paid by the creditor if repayment is made (and hence a penalty constituted by the non-payment in case of default). The bonus function is assumed to be a continuous, increasing function of the capital stock that the country ends the game with, equalling zero if the country ends the game with zero capital. Let $w(K, D)$ be the value to the debtor of pursuing an optimal plan for repaying an initial debt D, given an initial capital stock K and assuming it will not get any debt forgiveness in the future, and $v(K)$ utility under the assumption that the debtor will never repay (i.e., financial autarchy).

They then define the value ϑ which is the amount of debt forgiveness that makes the debtor indifferent between pursuing its optimal repayment strategy given that it expects no future debt forgiveness, and following the optimal strategy with no repayment ever of the debt. Thus, ϑ is defined implicitly from

$$w(K, D - \vartheta) = v(K).$$

It turns out that the unique subgame perfect equilibrium has the creditor offering debt forgiveness equal to ϑ in the first period, and the debtor thereafter repaying the debt optimally without further debt forgiveness. The solution is surprising because one would expect that the debtor would distort the investment path in order to get further debt forgiveness. The answer is that it can, but that it is not in its self-interest since it is making itself worse off.

Unfortunately, actual debt renegotiations have not been so smooth, and one of the factors has been that the creditors do not act as one. Heterogeneity among creditors in the context of a stochastic income stream is considered next.

Chapter 9

Uncertainty and Credit Rationing

9.1. Basic Issues

The last chapter considered some simple models of sovereign lending, showing that in general the incentives for repayment on the part of a borrower would not support the first-best optimal amount of lending, since in the absence of any additional default penalty the borrower would not have any incentive to repay if he did not face the prospect of borrowing again. However, if income fluctuated the borrower might want to retain access to borrowing in order to smooth consumption in the future. That incentive compatibility constraint could support positive lending (under certain conditions) but at a lower level of debt than the optimal one, provided that the borrower did not have access to a storage technology that permitted him to smooth consumption without borrowing. In the latter case of a riskless storage technology, potential lenders would not in fact lend, knowing that the borrower would default.

However, the last chapter also cast doubt on the assumption that defaulting borrowers would be shut out from capital markets forever. Since bygones are bygones, it is not clear that the subsequent incentives facing the lender would lead him to deny any future loans to a borrower who had defaulted in the past.

The models we considered also did not allow for a feedback of the stock of the debt on the subsequent investment (and other) decisions of the borrower — a possibility that arose naturally in the context of the 1980s debt crisis, as the borrowing countries had little incentive to undertake productive investments if the returns on those investments simply went to pay off creditors. Hence the push on the part of governments to get lenders to formally write down their debts (renouncing any further legal recourse). This led to the Brady plan which coordinated debt write-downs, replacing bank debt by new bonds with a lower principal amount, but collaterised with US treasury securities.

The models of this chapter thus introduce some additional complications. First, we allow the return on investment (or alternatively, the cost of defaulting) to be stochastic. Second, we allow for lenders to ration credit. This can easily be justified in terms of the models of the last chapter, since the stock of debt that borrowers would want to take on exceeded the amount consistent with repayment. However, here we consider not a single lender but a continuum of them, and this raises issues of monitoring the total size of loans and also the possibility that some creditors would be paid off, but others not. Finally, we allow for the possibility that "effort" on the part of the borrower (which could include willingness to undertake productive investment) could be endogenous and could depend on the debt level.

9.2. Exogenous Effort but Stochastic Costs of Default

9.2.1. *A benchmark case: Riskless lending*

Following Eaton and Fernandez (1995), we assume that a country gets a gross pay-off $W(L)$ from borrowing amount L at rate $R(L)$. Note that the interest rate is allowed to vary with the total amount loaned — in general, positively. Assume $W' > 0$, $W'' < 0$. Risk neutral lenders have access to an international capital market at which they can borrow or lend at the riskless rate r. So perfect competition among lenders reduces the expected return on sovereign lending to rate r.

Thus, if there is no risk of default (perfect enforcement of debt repayment), then

$$R(L) = r,$$

and the optimal amount of borrowing by the developing country will be given by

$$W'(L) = r.$$

Thus, the gross benefit from borrowing must equal the gross riskless rate. This is the benchmark case, against which more realistic cases that involve risk of default will be compared.

9.2.2. *Credit rationing with shared debt forgiveness*

But assume that the cost per loan unit to the borrower of not meeting its obligations is H, which may not be known when the loan was made. It is assumed to be drawn from a cumulative distribution $F(H)$ [with probability density function $F'(H)$]. H has mean $\overline{H}$. If $H > D$, where $D = RL$ are the repayment obligations, the debtor repays everything; but if $D > H$, then the debtor renegotiates the debt, repaying H, and does not incur any additional penalty. All creditors are assumed to be on the same footing here, and they share equally the repayments.

In this case, the debtor's net pay-off is

$$W(L) - D\left[1 - F(D)\right] - \int_0^D H dF(H). \tag{9.1}$$

The second term is the debt obligation times the probability that $H > D$, and hence the debt is fully repaid; the third term is the expected value of partial repayment. Competition among lenders ensures that the expected pay-off per unit of debt L is once again equal to the riskless rate:

$$R(L)\left[1 - F(D)\right] + \frac{1}{L}\int_0^D H dF(H) = r. \tag{9.2}$$

If lenders set both the rate and quantity of loans so as to satisfy the zero profit condition (9.2) and maximise the debtor's net pay-off (9.1), then once again the optimal level of lending and borrowing occurs. We can see this by substituting (9.2) into (9.1) (noting $D = RL$) and maximising with respect to L, giving a level of lending L^* such that $W'(L^*) = r$.

So this set-up once again gives the optimal amount of lending.

9.2.3.   *Lenders do not ration credit*

Consider the more realistic case where lenders set the rate at which they will loan money, but do not set the quantity, which is determined by the borrower after the rate is set. The interest rate is thus set to satisfy (9.2), and then the borrower decides the loan quantity so as to maximise net gain (9.1), taking the interest rate as given. Letting $\overline{R}$ be that interest rate, the borrower maximises

$$W(L) - \overline{R}L[1 - F(\overline{R}L)] - \int_0^{\overline{R}L} H dF(H),$$

giving the first-order condition [noting that $dF(H) = F'(H)dH$]

$$W'(L) - \overline{R}\left[1 - F(\overline{R}L)\right] + \overline{R}DF'(D) - \overline{R}DF'(D) = 0.$$

So, from (9.2)

$$W'(L) = \overline{R}[1 - F(\overline{R}L)] = r - \frac{1}{L}\int_0^D H dF(H) < r. \qquad (9.3)$$

So here there is overborrowing, pushing down the rate of return on loans below the world riskless rate. The reason is that each increment to borrowing increases the risk of default, but does not affect the borrower's costs. This is true because if the borrower defaults, it only repays the lenders up to the amount of its "penalty", and defaults on the rest (without additional penalty). Costless renegotiation of the debt occurs.

In essence, this is an example of moral hazard, with the risks being shifted from the borrower to the lender. Since the latter has set its interest rate first, and the quantity is fixed by the borrower, there is a distortion in international lending markets. This may have described the period of petrodollar recycling in the 1970s to early 1980s, as banks were not aware of the total amount of borrowing that was done with other lenders, the country arranging deals separately with individual banks (or syndicates of banks). After this period, there was a much more serious attempt to collect the relevant data on total debt exposures of developing countries. It is also true that shifts from bank lending to bond issues on international markets, which occurred after the 1980s, facilitated transparency since the size and terms of the issue were matters of public record (they typically have to be registered with national security commissions). But, as we will see later, having a large number of dispersed bond holders generates other issues, for instance collective action problems.

9.2.4. *Rationing with potential penalisation*

Assume now that the debt contracts cannot be renegotiated, but that failure to live up to the contract causes the borrower to suffer a default penalty, whatever the amount of its (partial) repayment. In these circumstances, if it defaults, it will have no incentive to pay anything, so that the choices are between full and zero repayment. So the expected payment to creditors is simply

$$Y = D[1 - F(D)].$$

It is important to note that the amount repaid may decrease with increasing debt, if (and only if)

$$\frac{dY}{dD} = 1 - F(D) - DF'(D) < 0. \tag{9.4}$$

In particular, if the default probability increases greatly with additional debt, then it could offset the higher contractual debt obligation and lead to lower repayment to the lender. This is only likely to occur at very high levels of debt, and, clearly, this is a perverse case, termed by Krugman (1988) the wrong side of the "Debt Laffer curve" (after the famous contention of Arthur Laffer that higher taxes lowered tax revenue). In more complicated models, this possibility is made plausible by pointing out that higher debt imposes perverse incentives on developing country borrowers: it may reduce investment, thus reducing the future resources available for repayment, and the higher taxes that residents anticipate having to pay in order for their government to service the debt may lead to capital flight. We will not explicitly model those linkages here.

Now once again we will assume that lenders set the interest rate and also ration credit such as to maximise the borrower's net gain subject to a zero profit condition for lenders, namely

$$R(L)\left[1 - F(D)\right] = r. \tag{9.5}$$

The pay-off to the borrower is once again Equation (9.1), which after substituting in (9.5) can be written as

$$W(L) - rL - \int_0^{R(L)L} H\,dF(H). \tag{9.6}$$

Maximising with respect to the loan amount gives the first-order condition

$$W'(L) - r - [R(L) + R'(L)L]DF'(D) = 0. \qquad (9.7)$$

Substitution for $R(L)$ using (9.5) into (9.7) gives

$$W'(L) = \frac{r[1 - F(D)]}{1 - F(D) - DF'(D)} > r. \qquad (9.8)$$

In this case the loan amount is below the optimal level that would equate the return to the riskless rate. Thus, the fact that the borrower in case of non-repayment pays a penalty that does not go to the lender provides an incentive for the latter to restrict credit below its optimal amount.

9.2.5. *Summary*

It is clear that the exact relationship between the borrower and the lender is crucial to the issue of whether there is overborrowing or not, whether there are actual defaults or just the threat of them, etc. No general conclusions have emerged, though many of the theoretical articles in the literature have sharp implications for various issues, for instance, whether there is a "debt overhang" (being on the wrong side of the debt Laffer curve), whether debt paybacks are in the interest of the borrowing countries (facing a very discounted market price for their debt which reflect expectations of default), etc. Some empirical work has thrown doubt on the debt Laffer curve, since it does not find that higher debt was associated with a lower market value. Also, despite theoretical objections by Bulow and Rogoff (1989), debt buy-backs in practice were pursued, seemingly with favourable results, by a number of developing countries during the debt crisis of the 1980s.

9.3.   Endogenous Effort on the Part of the Borrower

9.3.1.   *Debt overhang*

The idea that a debt overhang may affect the incentives to increase capacity to repay can be captured in an expanded model, where both the gross pay-off and the default probability (i.e., the distribution of H) depend on some potentially unobserved effort γ on the part of the borrowing country. We assume that the lender sets both the interest rate and the loan amount. Net benefits W are concave in effort, and we assume that ignoring debt considerations, there is an interior maximum for effort, $\gamma = \gamma^*$. The default probability depends negatively on effort and is concave. Since F is decreasing in γ, an increase in γ corresponds to a rightward shift of the distribution of H; so the likelihood of values of the default penalty above the contractual debt has increased. Therefore, the debtor will have a greater incentive to repay. Now, the borrower's net pay-off is

$$W(L, \gamma) - D[1 - F(D, \gamma)] - \int_0^D H F_H(H, \gamma) dH. \qquad (9.9)$$

The lender's zero profit condition becomes

$$R[1 - F(D, \gamma)] + \frac{1}{L} \int_0^D H F_H(H, \gamma) dH = r, \qquad (9.10)$$

and it can be shown that the credit terms that the lender is willing to give improve as a function of effort taken by the borrower. However, the effort may occur after the loan is made, and the borrower may not be able to precommit to a particular level of effort.

9.3.2.   *Precommitment*

Let us look at the case where the borrower can precommit to a particular level of effort. It will choose the level of effort to influence the terms set by the lender, where greater effort lowers the borrowing cost. The lender will set the rate subject to the zero profit condition, Equation (9.10). In these circumstances, the borrower will choose optimal effort, and the lender will supply the optimal amount of credit, the two satisfying

$$W_H(L^*, \gamma^*) = r,$$
$$W_\gamma(L^*, \gamma^*) = 0.$$

9.3.3. *Lack of commitment*

The more realistic case makes the choice of effort occur after the loan is granted and assumes no ability of the borrower to precommit. So effort is decided when both R and L are given, and the borrower ignores the impact that effort would have had on them. The borrower's first-order condition is now

$$W_\gamma = -\int_0^D F_\gamma(H, \gamma) dH. \tag{9.11}$$

The RHS is positive, hence so is the partial derivative of the gross benefit W. Therefore, effort is below the internal maximum γ^*. The intuition is as follows: if the borrower chooses effort after the loan terms have been agreed, then it takes actions to reduce the expected cost of default, and this reduces the incentive to repay once the draw for H is made. As a result, the lender will restrict credit below the optimal precommitment regime level.

This framework can be used to understand the possible effects of a debt overhang, where investment suffers because the decision-makers in the borrowing country know that though increased effort increases the net pay-off, it also increases the repayment probability (so essentially their returns will be taxed away). The framework can also be used to study the effect of international institutions in facilitating lending to developing countries or resolving debt crises. These (and other) issues are considered in the next chapter.

Chapter 10

Conclusion: Challenges to the International Monetary System and Prospects for Reform

10.1. Relevance of the Analysis for the Future

The history of the past few decades, on which we have drawn repeatedly to explain the development of economic theory on currency crises, coordination, currency unions, and sovereign debt, has highlighted inadequacies in the international monetary system. Currency and balance of payments crises have had enormous costs, and measures taken to contain them seem to have had limited effectiveness. Policy coordination has been episodic, both at the international and at the regional level. Indeed, the high point of G-7 policy coordination is widely viewed as having been reached in the period from the late 1970s to mid-1980s, while the high hopes for coordination of fiscal policies under the auspices the European Union's Excessive Deficits Procedures and Stability and Growth Pact have largely been disappointed. Sovereign defaults, far from being a thing of the past, have reappeared with a vengeance with the largest default in history, Argentina's 2001 default on $100 billion of external debt and its 2005 settlement of claims for only 30 percent of face value. Thus, despite some changes to the international environment in the light of the problems mentioned above, this concluding chapter will argue that the economic analysis of this book will continue to be a key tool for understanding the operation and further evolution of the international monetary system.

10.2. Recent Changes to the Environment for International Finance

Lessons have been drawn from the failures of the international monetary system, and they have led to important changes in several areas. In particular, first, currency regimes have evolved in a way that makes countries less vulnerable to crises. Second, private financing of developing countries has continued to develop, reducing spreads and leading to a maturing of the market for emerging market bonds. Third, official financing and official involvement in the resolution of crises have become much less significant.

10.2.1. *Exchange rate regimes*

Exchange rate regimes have to some extent evolved towards the polar cases of pure floats or hard fixes. The more financially advanced developing countries — often called "emerging market economies" — have moved away from adjustable exchange rate pegs (official or unofficial) to accept greater exchange rate flexibility. This is true of almost all of the major crisis countries. Mexico, Brazil, and Argentina are all operating flexible exchange rate regimes with inflation targeting providing the domestic monetary anchor. In Asia, Indonesia, Korea, and Thailand no longer have de facto pegs, though there is some intervention so that the currency does not float freely. China has announced the intention to accept greater flexibility, though to date currency fluctuations have been small. The exceptions to the Asian trend towards greater flexibility include Hong Kong, which continues to operate a currency board, and Malaysia, with an official dollar peg.

At the same time, the option of eliminating exchange rate volatility by forming a currency union has been put into practice in Europe, with the successful introduction of the euro in 1999, which to date has replaced national currencies for 13 of its member countries. The euro zone is slated to expand further, and it serves as a model for other regions that are contemplating introducing their own regional currencies. Projects for currency unions have been proposed for several regions in Africa (as well as, eventually, the African continent as a whole), the Gulf Cooperation Council, and East Asia, among others. Thus, common currency areas is likely to continue to be fertile ground for economists to analyse.

While moves toward either pure float or hard fix exchange rate regimes have the potential for reducing the incidence of crises, it is important to recognise the limitations of this trend. First, many developing countries do not want to accept the volatility involved in a pure float; hence they exhibit "fear of floating" by intervening, at times heavily. Second, an exchange rate peg may well continue to be attractive in special circumstances, for countries without monetary policy credibility, as a basis for "exchange rate based stabilisations". While countries like Chile, Mexico, and Brazil may have developed the track record for anti-inflation discipline and central bank independence in a generally benign international environment, inflation targeting regimes may be tested if the environment becomes less favourable, and other countries may not have achieved the same degree of credibility. Finally, it is by no means sure that the trend to greater flexibility is a durable one: the data in fact do not suggest that intermediate exchange rate regimes are in the process of being eliminated [see Masson (2001a)].

10.2.2. *The maturing of emerging market debt as an asset class*

In the past, lending to developing countries has been characterised by very high interest rates, periods of complete cut-off of lending and drying up of international debt markets ("sudden stops"), and contagion across countries during crisis episodes that did not seem to be justified by the economic circumstances of the affected country. Recent developments suggest a maturing of the asset class that makes it more similar to the markets for corporate bonds in advanced countries. Such an evolution would not be expected to eliminate crises but might make their occurrence less likely because they have become more closely linked to the objective ability of a country to service its debts, and less the result of self-fulfilling expectations or contagion from elsewhere.

The first decade of the current century has so far seen a steady and dramatic decline in emerging market spreads (Chart 10.1), which has occurred despite the unfavourable circumstances of Argentina's default. Indeed, there seems now to be much less evidence of the contagion that characterised the Mexican, Asian, and Russian crises. Investors have correctly considered events in Argentina to have little relevance to the possibility of a default by other emerging market borrowers. Greater differentiation should mean that the possibility that countries will be shut out from international borrowing is much less likely — unless they are themselves close to default for reasons particular to them.

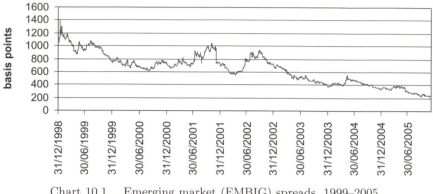

Chart 10.1. Emerging market (EMBIG) spreads, 1999–2005.
Source: JP Morgan.

10.2.3. *Reduction in the role of official institutions in resolving crises*

Just as the markets for private financing of developing countries have grown, so has the importance of official institutions declined. During the 1980s debt crises, the International Monetary Fund and the World Bank were the only source of financing for many developing countries, but at present, countries can borrow elsewhere if they do not want to submit themselves to the often onerous conditionality associated with the lending of the Bretton Woods institutions. The Asian crises provoked in many of the affected countries an aversion for the IMF's policy advice, and they have accumulated large stocks of international reserves to provide a cushion in case of balance of payments problems that would substitute for the need to borrow from the IMF. Brazil, Russia, and Argentina have all repaid in advance their IMF loans, incurred in recent years during balance of payments crises.

The fact that the IMF did not play any role in the settlement between Argentina and its creditors has encouraged many to believe that international organisations are not needed to resolve issues arising with sovereign debt. A somewhat extreme view is expressed by Mary Anastasia O'Grady in the *Wall Street Journal* (March 4, 2005):

> "the world may have moved a step closer to a market-driven financial system where the costs of malfeasance are shouldered by those who borrow and lend rather than socialized through the IMF. (...) Closing down the IMF may be too much to hope for. But it is at least important to note that Argentina provides two priceless lessons. The first is that IMF largess not only damages reform momentum but also exacerbates risk. The second is that borrowers and lenders can work out bond defaults on their own, and when they do, incentives are likely to return to the emerging markets, raising accountability in governance."

10.3. Continuing Challenges

History suggests that the relatively benign international environment prevailing in 2006 will not continue forever, and that the recent evolution of the international monetary system will not remove the need for new mechanisms and official interventions in the future. Thus, research into international economic cooperation and into the causes and prevention of currency and debt crises will return to prominence. Continuing challenges will lead to efforts at international cooperation and stimulate a search for a better way to operate the international monetary system. If the international environment ceases to be characterised by ample global liquidity, low inflation, and steady growth, countries may recognise the urgency of discussing changes to the international monetary system in order to minimise negative impacts. In addition to such short-run conjunctural factors, several structural problems will play a role in future in stimulating reform.

10.3.1. *The plight of the poorest countries*

While economic development at a dramatic pace has increased incomes in China, India, and some other developing countries, it has not reached the very poorest countries, principally those in Africa. While the failure of aid has been well documented (Easterly, 2002), it will be difficult for the world to be indifferent to the plight of Africa, continuing to stagnate as other regions grow, especially as the continent is being devastated by HIV/AIDS. The G-7 countries have subscribed to the Millennium Development Goals, which among other objectives target a reduction by half of the number of people in extreme poverty by 2015, and significant improvements in health and education. While the recent decision by the richest countries to forgive their loans, and those of the official institutions, to the poorest countries (in the context of the Heavily Indebted, Poor Country initiative), there is reluctance on the part of rich countries to increase lending in the future. Instead, loans are to be replaced by grants, and there is to be greater selectivity with respect to recipient countries. However, in reality the poorest countries often do not have the institutions to deliver good governance and implement the policies that would qualify them for the more stringent criteria that are now being asked of them as conditions for rich countries assistance. This dilemma will continue to provide challenges for advanced countries' and the Bretton Woods institutions' attempts to help the poorest countries, and may lead to the search for ways to channel private financing more effectively to poorer countries.

10.3.2. *Global imbalances*

At present, the world is in the paradoxical position that the world's richest country (at least by some measures), the United States, is running a capital account surplus and a current account deficit that is equal to about $800 billion dollars in 2006 (or 6 percent of US GDP). Moreover, the United States is already by far the world's largest debtor. Instead of flowing to developing countries where it can help them to catch up, a large amount of capital is going to the most advanced country so that it can live beyond its means (since the US current account has been fuelled mainly by strong consumption and housing demand in the United States, not investment). While economists disagree about the causes for that imbalance, and whether it is sustainable or not, many fear that it must be reversed at some point, and that its unwinding will involve a large depreciation of the US dollar. A depreciation of the dollar is not in itself a cause for concern, but a sharp and disruptive one, where the decline fed on itself and led to overshooting, could be extremely unsettling to international financial markets and could lead to a period of slow or negative growth, both in the United States and elsewhere.

A similar situation existed in an earlier period, the first half of the 1980s, when a combination of expansionary fiscal policy and tight monetary policy in the United States led to a large appreciation of the dollar and US fiscal and current account deficits. G5/G7 policy coordination (the Plaza Agreement and the Louvre Accord) helped to bring about an orderly decline of the value of the dollar, preventing harmful volatility. That coordination could provide a model for the second half-decade of the current century, but probably will not. The problem is that all the important players were included in the G7 in the earlier period, but the same is not true now. One of the major players now is China, since it runs a large current account surplus and the lack of flexibility of its exchange rate against the dollar impedes international adjustment. Other important players are the oil exporting countries, which are also running large current account surpluses.

Thus, the existing G7 framework is no longer adequate to handle the challenges for international economic policy coordination, and other fora need to be found. An obvious one is the IMF, since it has global membership, and it has recently been given a mandate by its largest shareholders (in particular, the United States) to conduct consultations with its members in order to reduce global imbalances. Time will tell whether this leads to an effective new role for the institution, since in principle the IMF has always had this responsibility. It may well be that the United States, China, and oil exporters will find no common ground for cooperation in this field, and the IMF no new leverage to force them to agree on solutions.

10.3.3.   *The decline in multilateralism*

A drawback for the IMF in promoting global cooperation is the weak legitimacy for international institutions generally. The IMF lost influence when its policy advice failed to fend off emerging market crises in Asia or Russia, and in Argentina its support is now widely viewed as having prolonged an unsustainable situation. While it is convenient for the Argentine authorities to blame the IMF, both its involvement with Argentina before the crisis and its lack of involvement in negotiating the terms of settlement with creditors have lowered its influence.

The IMF's sullied reputation in Asia has to do with its questionable policy advice during the crises but also with the inadequate representation of the region within the IMF's executive board. That issue is in the process of being at least partially addressed, but nevertheless has fuelled in the meantime moves towards regional integration as a substitute for multilateralism. Thus, ASEAN+3 (ASEAN, China, Japan, and Korea) is a forum for pooling foreign exchange reserves and for considering other aspects, such as a free trade area and exchange rate linkages.

The decline in multilateralism also is reflected in the (perhaps temporary) breakdown in the Doha Round negotiations of the WTO. Among the major players, the United States has made clear its distrust of international agreements and multilateral commitments, while the European Community has turned inward, as the admission of 10 new members in 2004 has created a backlash from the older members that led to a rejection of the European Constitution by referendums held in France and the Netherlands. In these circumstances, neither the United States nor the EU is willing to force farmers to make sacrifices in the interests of developing countries with little political influence. In the trade field, retreat from multilateralism has shown itself in a proliferation of bilateral or regional agreements, rather than continued progress towards global free trade.

10.4. Reform Proposals

At present, though there is no international bankruptcy law for sovereign lenders, the IMF, the World Bank, and other international organisations provide loans to developing countries and attempt to resolve situations where borrowers cannot or will not repay. The mandate of the IMF, for instance, states that it should provide financial assistance to prevent a severe fall in output that might accompany a country's need to adjust its balance of payments to make it sustainable.[1] However, this mandate was designed for a world where countries did not have access to world capital markets (i.e., faced a current account crisis, not one of withdrawal of capital). When a country has liberalised its capital account, it is subject to balance of payments outflows that are potentially much larger than those associated with an unsustainable current account deficit. A number of proposals have been made to improve the functioning of the international monetary system in the environment of open capital markets, and there is an extensive theoretical literature trying to analyse these institutions. Proposals to reform the international monetary system have been variants of three quite different approaches: (i) create an international bankruptcy tribunal that would do what Chapter 11

---

[1] Article I(v) of the IMF's Articles of Agreement lists among the purposes of the organisation, "To give confidence to members by making the general resources of the Fund temporarily available to them under adequate safeguards, thus providing them with opportunity to correct maladjustments in their balance of payments without resorting to measures destructive of national or international prosperity".

does for US commercial borrowers; (ii) create an international lender of last resort (LOLR); and (iii) improve the terms of loan/bond contracts so that private lenders can overcome collective action problems and resolve debt problems themselves. The models discussed in this book help to shed light on these proposals.

10.4.1. *The rationale for the existing role of the IMF*

At present, the IMF lends money to developing countries that have run into problems, subject to commitments by the countries to make necessary improvements in their policies ("conditionality"). The loans are phased, and the later disbursements are subject to review; if the policy commitments have not been taken, then the IMF will not authorise further payments.

The exercise of conditionality by the IMF can be modelled as a monitoring technology that allows countries to precommit to effort that improves their chances of repayment as well as moves effort closer to its optimal level. Recall from Section 9.2.2 that with precommitment, countries attain their first-best level of lending. With the IMF's conditionality in place (i.e., an agreed IMF program), private lenders are often willing to resume lending. Thus, the IMF helps to reduce the distortions in the incentives on debtor countries to furnish effort, and this stimulates lending to them.

Another approach [due to Marchesi and Thomas (1999)] sees the IMF program as a signalling device that indicates the true intentions of the developing country borrower. By submitting itself to the pain of an IMF program it shows that it is serious about reform and debt repayment. So this is another surrogate for precommitment.

Though seemingly large in absolute terms, the IMF's resources are however dwarfed by the size of international capital flows. Thus, apologists of IMF lending have stressed its "catalytic role" stimulating other lending. In itself, it is unable to prevent crises or even to substitute for private lending — witness the sharp declines in output and severe financial crises suffered by the recipients of IMF lending (Mexico, Thailand, Indonesia, and Argentina). Moreover, the monitoring technology argument assumes that the IMF's policy recommendations are widely agreed to improve the country's economic outlook — something that has been contested in the light of weak evidence in favour of IMF program effectiveness.

The decline in the demand for IMF lending — referred to above — has put renewed emphasis on the ability of the institution to take a global perspective and provide cooperative solutions to problems, though it has no way of coercing countries to accept its advice. The quality of its advice will be particularly important if it is to persuade and facilitate solutions, rather than just being one of many global think tanks. Other roles however are possible that would give it once again in a central operational role the international system.

10.4.2. *A world bankruptcy tribunal for sovereign borrowers?*

This idea was floated by Jeffrey Sachs in his 1995 Graham lectures at Princeton University, and more recently advocated by Anne Krueger, former Deputy Managing Director of the IMF, in the form of a Sovereign Debt Restructuring Mechanism (SDRM). As demonstrated in the previous chapter, in some circumstances lack of enforceability of sovereign loan contracts limits the amount of lending to them, and heterogeneity among lenders makes resolution of debt crises difficult. The big advantage seen for a SDRM would be that it would make the resolution of defaults cleaner and avoid the long periods when there are disincentive effects from a debt overhang. It would also permit "debtor in possession financing", by analogy with domestic bankruptcy law, which gives incentives for new lending, since such new lending would be made senior to existing loans (that is, be repaid first).

The main objection to this idea, which has proved to be fatal to it, is the existence of legal complications: a treaty would have to be agreed to by all (or almost all) creditor nations to subordinate their national courts to an international bankruptcy court (so that Argentine bondholders could not go to a New York judge to get him to block a restructuring deal, for instance). In practice, the United States and some other major creditor countries are unwilling to do so. Other objections are that such a court would tilt the balance towards the debtor countries, and make default too easy — shifting to the left the distribution of costs of default $F(H)$ in the models discussed in Chapter 9 and thus reducing effort on the part of the borrower.

10.4.3.   *An international LOLR?*

There have been a few proposals for a dramatic increase in the funds available to the IMF or another international lender so that it could take on the role equivalent to that of a central bank in domestic financial markets [e.g., Fischer (1999)]. The rationale for doing so is the contention that emerging market debt crises are similar to bank runs in the domestic financial system [Sachs (1984)]: they are liquidity, not solvency crises, and lending money quickly (and probably with few conditions, but perhaps with collateral, as for a domestic LOLR) would improve world welfare. Going back to our earlier work on currency crises, this could be justified by second- or third-generation crisis models with multiple equilibria driven by investors' self-fulfilling expectations. Providing large amounts of funding could reverse a move to the bad equilibrium; the knowledge that the funds would be forthcoming would in fact prevent the crisis from occurring, since investors would not be in the prisoner's dilemma situation of knowing that if other investors ran and they did not, they would end up with large losses.

Objections to such an international LOLR take several forms. First, the amounts available to such an institution would have to be enormous, given the volume of international capital flows. A domestic central bank can create unlimited amounts of liquidity in a crisis, because it is the issuer of the currency. The same is not true of the IMF, which is not a world central bank. It is limited in its lending by the amounts paid in by member countries. Second, it has been argued that the moral hazard problems would be severe (and some argue already are severe from IMF bailouts): countries would not attempt to take measures to prevent crises (effort would be low, in the model given above), especially if IMF conditionality were made less onerous. Indeed, "prequalification", that is certifying that countries would have automatic access to a credit line in a crisis, would eliminate *ex post* conditionality completely. Third, some have maintained that a LOLR was fixing the wrong problem, namely distortions in international sovereign debt markets that needed to be addressed in other ways. This leads to a third reform proposal, on which some progress has been made.

10.4.4. *Changing the terms of loan contracts*

This more modest agenda has led to changes in the terms of issues of sovereign debt, extending the scope of "collective action clauses" (CACs), which help defaulting debtors reach agreement with their creditors. In particular, more and more sovereign debt contracts are being written with London terms rather than with those prevalent in New York, where a very large majority (often 95 percent or more) is needed to change the terms of the loan contract. New York terms make restructuring difficult and lengthen the time during which debt overhang occurs. London terms include CACs that make a simple majority (or a limited super majority) of bondholders sufficient to change the loan contract. Thus, these clauses would facilitate resolution of loan crises. However, they would do nothing to prevent them, and some have argued that they would exacerbate the likelihood that debtors would choose to default (or provide low effort, see above). Nevertheless, issuers who have included CACs recently have not in fact faced (much) higher interest rates, suggesting that the lenders are not overly concerned about the negative incentive effects.

10.5.   Whither International Financial Architecture?

The ambitious reform proposals have not borne fruit, though the inclusion of CACs should improve the way international loan markets work. It seems likely that there will be no dramatic changes in the international "rules of the game" in the near future. Argentina's 2005 restructuring of its external debt, done in the face of IMF disapproval but successful nonetheless, signals a period of partial disengagement of official institutions: borrowers and private lenders will be increasingly left to themselves to resolve debt crises.

A return to a situation where capital is much more controlled, as in the early post-war years — is also not going to occur. Although more freely mobile capital has risks — in particular opening the door to financial crises — it also has evident benefits. Though capital controls have garnered a few proponents, they are unlikely to prevail generally in the light of the technological changes that make taking positions against a currency or engineering capital flight relatively easy (e.g., through derivatives). There is much empirical evidence of the ineffectiveness of capital controls, with evasion becoming easier with the passage of time.

As discussed above, the greater prevalence of flexible exchange rates among emerging market economies has decreased vulnerability to speculative capital outflows. However, liquidity and solvency crises are still possible even when there is no exchange rate commitment. So the world is likely to face future international crises, either debt crises or currency crises, and continue to grope towards a better way of resolving them. The tools presented in this book will help in that endeavour.

Bibliography

Agénor, P-R and PR Masson (1999). Credibility, reputation, and the Mexican peso crisis. *Journal of Money, Credit and Banking*, 31, 70–84.

Agénor, P-R, M Miller, D Vines and A Weber (eds.) (1999). *The Asian Financial Crisis: Causes, Contagion and Consequences*. Cambridge, UK: Cambridge University Press.

Aghion, P, P Bacchetta and A Banerjee (2001). Currency crises and monetary policy in an economy with credit constraints. *European Economic Review*, 45(7), 1121–1150.

Aghion, P, P Bacchetta and A Banerjee (2004). Financial development and the instability of open economies. *Journal of Monetary Economics*, 51, 1077–1106.

Alba, P, A Bhattacharya, S Claessens, S Ghosh and L Hernandez (1999). The role of macroeconomic and financial sector linkages in east Asia's financial crisis. In *The Asian Financial Crisis: Causes, Contagion and Consequences*, P-R Agenor, M Miller, D Vines and A Weber (eds.). Cambridge University Press.

Alesina, A and R Barro (2002). Currency unions. *Quarterly Journal of Economics*, 117, 409–436.

Alesina, A and G Tabellini (1987). Rules and discretion with noncoordinated monetary and fiscal policies. *Economic Inquiry*, 25, 619–630.

Banerjee, A (1992). A simple model of herd behavior. *Quarterly Journal of Economics*, 107, 797–817.

Barro, R and D Gordon (1983). Rules, discretion and reputation in a model of monetary policy. *Journal of Monetary Economics*, 12, 101–121.

Beetsma, R and L Bovenberg (1998). Monetary union without fiscal coordination may discipline policymakers. *Journal of International Economics*, 45, 239–258.

Beetsma, R and X Debrun (2004). The interaction between monetary and fiscal policies in a monetary union: A review of recent literature. In *Fiscal Policies, Monetary Policies and Labour Markets: Key Aspects of European Macroeconomic Policies After Monetary Unification*, R Beetsma *et al.* (eds.). Cambridge, UK: Cambridge University Press.

Bikchandani, S, D Hirshleifer and I Welch (1992). A theory of fads, fashion, custom, and cultural change as informational cascades. *Journal of Political Economy*, 100(5), 992–1026.

Blanco, H and PM Garber (1986). Recurrent devaluation and speculative attacks on the Mexican peso. *Journal of Political Economy*, 94(1), 148–166.

Brainard, W (1967). Uncertainty and the effectiveness of policy. *American Economic Review*, 57, 411–425.

Broner, F (forthcoming) Discrete devaluations and multiple equilibria in a first generation model of currency crises. *Journal of Monetary Economics*.

Buiter, W and R Marston (eds.) (1984). *International Economic Policy Coordination*. Cambridge University Press.

Bulow, J and K Rogoff (1989). LDC debt: Is to forgive to forget? *American Economic Review*, 79(1), 43–50.

Camerer, CF (1997). Progress in behavioral game theory. *Journal of Economic Perspectives*, 11, 167–188.

Canzoneri, M and J Gray (1985). Monetary policy games and the consequencs of non-cooperative behavior. *International Economic Review*, 26(3), 547–564.

Canzoneri, MB and D Henderson (1991). *Monetary Policy in Interdependent Economies: A Game Theoretic Approach*. MIT Press.

Cole, H and T Kehoe (1996). A self-fulfilling model of Mexico's 1994–95 debt crisis. *Journal of International Economics*, 41, 309–330.

Cooper, RN (1985). Economic interdependencies and coordination of policies. In *Handbook of International Economics*, R Jones and P Kenen (eds.) Vol. 2, pp. 1195–1234. Amsterdam: North-Holland.

Debrun, X and PR Masson (2005). Monetary union, dollarization, and independent currencies — a unified treatment. Mimeo.

Debrun, X, PR Masson and C Pattillo (2005). Monetary unions in West Africa: Who might gain, who might lose and why? *Canadian Journal of Economics*, 38, 454–481.

Drazen, A (2000). *Political Economy in Macroeconomics*. Princeton.

Drazen, A and PR Masson (1994). Credibility of policies versus credibility of policymakers. *Quarterly Journal of Economics*, 109, 735–754.

Easterly, W (2002). *The Elusive Quest for Growth: Economists' Adventures and Misadventures in the Tropics*. Cambridge, MA: MIT Press.

Eaton, J and R Fernandez (1995). Sovereign debt. In *Handbook of International Economics*, Vol. 3, G Grossman and K Rogoff (eds.), pp. 2031–2077. New York: Elsevier.

Eaton, J and M Gersovitz (1981). Debt with potential repudiation: Theoretical and empirical analysis. *Review of Economic Studies*, 48(2), 289–309.

Eichengreen, B (1999). *Toward a New Financial Architecture: A Practical Post-Asia Agenda*. Washington, DC: Institute of International Economics.

Eichengreen, B, A Rose and C Wyplosz (1995). Exchange market mayhem: The antecedents and aftermath of speculative attacks. *Economic Policy*, pp. 251–296.

Fischer, S (1999). On the need for an international lender of last resort. *Journal of Economic Perspectives*, 13(4), 85–104.

Flood, RP and PM Garber (1994). Collapsing exchange-rate regimes: Some linear examples. *Journal of International Economics*, 16, 1–13. Reprinted in Flood and Garber (1994).

Flood, RP and PM Garber (1994). *Speculative Bubbles, Speculative Attacks, and Policy Switching*. Cambridge, MA: MIT Press.

Flood, RP and NP Marion (2000). Self-fulfilling risk predictions: An application to speculative attacks. *Journal of International Economics*, 50(1), 245–268.

Forbes, K and R Rigobon (2002). No contagion, only interdependence: Measuring stock market comovements. *Journal of Finance*, 57, 2223–2261.

Frankel, J and K Rockett (1988). International macroeconomic policy coordination when policymakers do not agree on the true model. *American Economic Review*, 78, 318–340.

Ghosh, A and PR Masson (1994). *Economic Cooperation in an Uncertain World*. Oxford, UK: Blackwell.

Glick, R, R Moreno and M Spiegel (eds.) (2001) *Financial Crises in Emerging Markets*. Cambridge, UK: Cambridge University Press.

Hamada, K (1976). A strategic analysis for monetary interdependence. *Journal of Political Economy*, 84, 677–700.

Helliwell, JF and T Padmore (1985). Empirical studies of macroeconomic interdependence. In *Handbook of International Economics*, RW Jones and PB Kenen (eds.) Vol. 3, Chapter 21, pp. 1107–1151. Elsevier.

Hellwig, C, A Mukherji and A Tsyvinski (2005). Self-fulfilling currency crises: The role of interest rates. NBER Working Paper 11191, National Bureau of Economic Research, Cambridge, MA.

Horne, J and PR Masson (1988). Scope and limits of international economic cooperation and policy coordination. *IMF Staff Papers*, 35, 259–296.

IMF (1993). *World Economic Outlook*. International Monetary Fund.

IMF (2004). *Evaluation Report: The IMF and Argentina, 1991–2001*. Independent Evaluation Office, International Monetary Fund.

James, H (1996). *International Monetary Cooperation Since Bretton Woods*. International Monetary Fund and Oxford University Press.

Jeanne, O (1997). Are currency crises self-fulfilling? A test. *Journal of International Economics*, 43, 263–286.

Jeanne, O and PR Masson (1996). Was the French Franc crisis a sunspot equilibrium? Mimeo, International Monetary Fund.

Jeanne, O and PR Masson (2000). Currency crises, sunspots and Markov-switching regimes. *Journal of International Economics*, 50, 327–350.

Komulainen, T (2004). *Essays on Financial Crises in Emerging Markets*, Bank of Finland Studies, Vol. E:29. PhD thesis, Turku School of Economics and Business Administration.

Krugman, PR (1979). A model of balance of payments crises. *Journal of Money, Credit and Banking*, 11(3), 311–325.

Krugman, PR (1988). Financing vs. forgiving a debt overhang: Some analytic notes. *Journal of Development Economics*, 29, 253–268.

Marchesi, S and JP Thomas (1999). IMF conditionality as a screening device. *Economic Journal*, 109, C111–C125.

Masson, PR (1992). Portfolio preference uncertainty and gains from policy coordination. *IMF Staff Papers*, 39(1), 101–120.

Masson, PR (1999a). Contagion: Macroeconomic models with multiple equilibria. *Journal of International Money and Finance*, 18(4), 587–602.

Masson, PR (1999b). Contagion: Monsoonal effects, spillovers, and jumps between multiple equilibria. In *The Asian Financial Crisis: Causes, Contagion and Consequences*, P-R Agénor, M Miller, D Vines and A Weber (eds.), pp. 265–280. Cambridge, UK: Cambridge University Press.

Masson, PR (2001a). Exchange rate regime transitions. *Journal of Development Economics*, 64, 571–586.

Masson, PR (2001b). Multiple equilibria, contagion, and emerging market crises. In *Financial Crises in Emerging Market*, R Glick, R Moreno and MM Spiegel (eds.), pp. 73–98. Cambridge, UK: Cambridge University Press.

Masson, PR and C Pattillo (2004). *The Monetary Geography of Africa*. Washington, DC: Brookings Institution.

McKibbin, W (1997). Empirical evidence on international economic policy coordination. In *Handbook of Comparative Economic Policies*, M Fratianni, D Salvatore and J Von Hagen (eds.), Vol. 5. Westport, CT: Greenwood Press.

Meyer, L, B Doyle, J Gagnon and D Henderson (2002). International coordination of macroeconomic policies: Still alive in the new millenium? *International Finance Discussion Papers*, 723. Board of Governors of the Federal Reserve System.

Morris, S and HS Shin (1998). Unique equilibrium in a model of self-fulfilling currency attacks. *American Economic Review*, 88, 587–597.

Morris, S and HS Shin (2002). Rethinking multiple equilibria in macroeconomic modeling. In *NBER Macroeconomics Annual*, Cambridge, MA, 2002. National Bureau of Economic Research. Comments by A Atkeson and H Rey.

Mundell, R (1961). A theory of optimum currency areas. *American Economic Review*, 51, 657–665.

Mussa, M (2002). *Argentina and the Fund: From Triumph to Tragedy*. Institute for International Economics.

Obstfeld, M (1984). Balance of payments crises and devaluation. *Journal of Money, Credit and Banking*, 16, 208–217.

Obstfeld, M (1994). The logic of currency crises. *Cahiers Economiques et Monetaires*, 43(43), 189–213.

Obstfeld, M (1996). Models of currency crises with self-fulfilling features. *European Economic Review*, 40, 1037–1048.

Oudiz, G and J Sachs (1984). Macroeconomic policy coordination among the industrial countries. *Brookings Papers on Economic Activity*, 1, 1–64.

Persson, T and G Tabellini (1995). Double-edged incentives: Institutions and policy coordination. In *Handbook of International Economics*, G Grossman and K Rogoff (eds.), Vol. 3, pp. 1973–2030. North-Holland.

Pesenti, P (2001) Discussion. In *Financial Crises in Emerging Markets*, R Glick, R Moreno and MM Spiegel (eds.), pp. 99–105. Cambridge, UK: Cambridge University Press.

Sachs, J (1984). Theoretical issues in international borrowing. *Princeton Studies in International Finance*, 54.

Salant, SW and DW Henderson (1978). Market anticipation of government policy and the price of gold. *Journal of Political Economy*, 86, 627–648.

Sarno, L and MP Taylor (2002). *The Economics of Exchange Rates*. Cambridge, UK: Cambridge University Press.

Triffin, R (1960). *Gold and the Dollar Crisis: The Future of Convertibility*. New Haven, CT: Yale University Press.

Woodford, M (1995). Price level determinacy without control of a monetary aggregate. *Carnegie-Rochester Conference Series on Public Policy*, 43, 1–46.

Index